I appreciate Luis Palau for bringing so many people together in fellowship and in celebration of faith, family, and values.

—**President George W. Bush**

I remember the first time I saw Luis. . . . What struck me was his genuine sense of concern for every person he came in touch with. It's something you can't fake. He's real.

—**President Bill Clinton**

God has used Luis in a tremendous way through many years. His friendship and support of me meant more than he will ever know.

—**The late Billy Graham**

It's obvious God has used Luis in a great way to fulfill His purposed for the Kingdom. I thank him for modeling that which matters most—transforming our world by changing lives through the abundant life found in Christ.

—**Rick Warren,** *New York Times* bestselling
author of *The Purpose Driven Life*

Words cannot express the deep appreciation I have for Luis and the fine work God has called him to do. His faithfulness in proclaiming God's glorious gospel across racial, cultural, and geographical lines has been nothing short of praiseworthy.

—**Tony Evans**

One of my greatest joys of my life ministry has been to be a part of Luis Palau's festivals. I love so much the man . . . and the passion of the man . . . Luis Palau.

—**Steven Curtis Chapman,** Grammy-award
winning recording artist

Every time I get the chance to do something with Luis . . . every time I get to sit with him . . . I come away inspired. He's an amazing evangelist. An amazing man. And a friend of mine. We thank God for the gift of Luis Palau. I, with countless thousands of others, came to Christ through Luis and his ministry.

—**Matt Redman,** Grammy-award winning recording artist

Luis Palau is a great evangelist and a close friend of my father. He has faithfully preached the Gospel around the world for over fifty years. I'm so grateful for this man's life and for his wonderful family.

—**Franklin Graham**

I deeply appreciate Luis's passionate dedication to spreading the Gospel. It would be impossible to measure his impact on Christendom throughout the past five decades as he has shared the Good News with folks around the world.

—**James Dobson**

I have great respect for Luis Palau. God has used him mightily over the years! I am blessed to consider him my friend.

—**Bishop M. V. Kelsey**

Palau

Also by Luis Palau

Changed by Faith (with Jay Fordice)

*A Friendly Dialogue Between an Atheist and
a Christian* (with Zhao Qizheng)

God Is Relevant (with David Sanford)

Healthy Habits for Spiritual Growth

High Definition Life (with Steve Halliday)

The Only Hope for America

Telling the Story (with Timothy Robnett)

Out of the Desert . . . Into the Life God Fully Intended

Where Is God When Bad Things Happen?

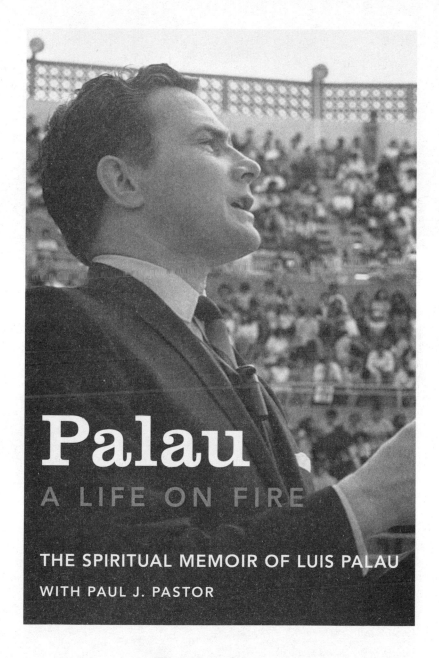

Palau
A LIFE ON FIRE

THE SPIRITUAL MEMOIR OF LUIS PALAU
WITH PAUL J. PASTOR

ZONDERVAN®

ZONDERVAN

Palau
Copyright © 2019 by Palau Family Trust

ISBN 978-0-310-35405-5 (hardcover)

ISBN 978-0-310-35560-1 (international trade paper edition)

ISBN 978-0-310-35407-9 (audio)

ISBN 978-0-310-35406-2 (ebook)

Requests for information should be addressed to:
Zondervan, 3900 *Sparks Dr. SE, Grand Rapids, Michigan 49546*

Published in association with the literary agency of D. C. Jacobson & Associates, LLC, an Author Management Company. www.dcjacobson.com.

Cover image: Luis Palau Association
Art direction: Curt Diepenhorst
Interior design: Denise Froehlich

Printed in the United States of America

19 20 21 22 23 /LSC/ 10 9 8 7 6 5 4 3 2 1

For Pat

Contents

Preface

Working on a book like this is a bit like painting an old-fashioned portrait. An artist (the writer) joins their subject for a series of sittings. Over the course of those hours, sketches are made, angles are considered, until the right presentation is found, that magic combination of subject and style that make you say *Yes! That's them!* It captures a life not in its entirety but in a way that suggests the whole.

Participating in the writing of this book was a unique honor. In Luis, I found a fascinating subject. Sharp, well-read, quick with a joke, deeply sincere. To get to know him in the intimate way that I did has been one of the great privileges of my life. Luis is a unique soul, a man of uncommon clarity of purpose. In a world of people unmoored from their sense of "why," Luis's calling rises with incredible sharpness. He is here to preach Christ crucified, the hope of glory. That is *all*.

This book posed a unique challenge. Though he'd be quick to downplay it, Luis Palau was a significant figure of twentieth-century history and life. His work impacted nations, shaped cultures, and transformed the spiritual and moral ecology of entire regions of the world. A comprehensive biography would take hundreds of pages more and risk obscuring the real man, the real Christian whose story it is.

11

We decided that the best gift we could offer you as a reader was the sense that you had sat down with him as I did. That he'd opened his front door, made you some coffee, set a plate of Pat's cookies in front of you (next to a bowl of the macadamia nuts he loves), and simply begun talking. You would not only hear the stories. You'd hear the lessons with them—and all through the people God used in his life.

This format has demanded hard choices. Do we get to tell the full story of how Luis's call-in television show helped stall a Marxist revolution in Ecuador? Alas, no. How about the time he got stuck in a Beijing elevator with the president of the United States? Nope. The story of *another* elevator ride where he helped shelter the Beatle George Harrison from a miniature mob chasing him down a hotel corridor? Sorry. I could go on for hours. Many of the juiciest tidbits are left behind. There's just too much. This isn't about the rhinestones of his life. It's about the diamonds.

Luis's heart is that this book would not leave you thinking, *Wow, Palau was a rock star.* He wants you to see a vision of Christ. He wants you to honor the unknown heroes of his life and work and to think about your own heroes. He wants the attention focused where it belongs: Jesus.

After one of our last interviews, Luis walked me out to my car. It was a spring morning. There were cherry blossoms on the trees. As we enjoyed the sun, I saw tears come into Luis's eyes. Suddenly, he pointed at the houses surrounding us in his Portland neighborhood. "So many of them don't know how *good* life is with Jesus," he said. "It's not just about the next life. They are missing out on His love *now*." There, in his driveway, he nearly began to weep. He *ached* for his neighbors. This man's heart burns for one thing: that all might have a chance to say yes to true life. And I began to tear up too—cut to the heart by the presence of true tenderness.

Enjoy this man's remarkable story.

PAUL J. PASTOR

Introduction

Trust in the Lord with all your heart
    and lean not on your own understanding;
in all your ways submit to him,
    and he will make your paths straight.

PROVERBS 3:5–6

You are holding a book that nearly was not written.

When I was diagnosed with incurable lung cancer in December of 2017, I was faced with the imminent reality that I have known and preached since I was a boy: the fact of death and the secure hope of eternal life in Jesus. Though I had the opportunity to write a book reflecting on my life, I was not at all sure that I wanted to spend my time that way—and *very* sure that I did *not* want to bring one atom of glory to my own name.

I have given my life to preaching the Good News that God loves all people and that the cross of Jesus Christ brings reconciliation and full assurance of eternal life to all who believe in Him and repent. The decades I spent doing this were very full. As my friends are quick to point out, I have traveled widely, spoken to many millions of people, and been instrumental in the work of the Holy Spirit to point hundreds of thousands of people to the saving cross of Jesus.

Now, in this final phase of my ministry, I fear drawing attention to myself. I feel—not just know but *feel*—the constant temptation of pride and ego. I feel the draw to puff myself up by means of telling my story. You must know that I fear that. The glory of my ministry does not belong to me.

I know for a fact that my work has been empowered by the sacrificial labor of countless others. These key people number in the hundreds—members of our team at the Luis Palau Association, our board of directors, generous donors, my own pastors and leaders, honest friends. A full telling of my story would mean a full telling of each of theirs, and how is that possible, short of eternity?

So I have tried to do the next best thing. I want to share the highlights of my story by drawing attention to key people in my life. In each chapter, I draw out one foundational lesson that relationship taught me. In this way, I hope this book will be more than the memoir of an old preacher—it is a book of biblical principles for living out the Good News. For that Good News places us in the loving arms of God, now and for eternity.

I want these chapters to remind us of the power of "unknown" lives. Very few people in this book are well known (Billy Graham being the exception). But they deserve to be honored. Each of them taught me something unique. These are people who will be exalted in heaven because they were humbly serving the Lord in their time and place.

If you are looking for a comprehensive biography of my life, listing all the places my team and I went, counting the world leaders we met, or expounding at length upon the numerical or historical impacts of our ministry, then this book will disappoint you. I have no interest in writing that book. Let's talk about that stuff when we catch up in the presence of Jesus someday.

Instead, I want you to feel that you have gotten to know me—the unfiltered me—and to know Jesus through my story. Introspection can be uncomfortable. But I hope my story draws out eternal lessons. With that in mind, I share my remembrances and reflections, hoping that the Holy Spirit will give you a sense of His power and that the things I have learned and experienced will point you to Jesus. In that way, my life story can be what I have always desired—a humble signpost pointing straight to God.

Let's begin with my prayer from the first time I met with Paul to begin the writing process:

Lord, help us exalt You and put all glory where it belongs— at the cross of our Lord Jesus Christ, without which we all would be lost. We thank You for the mercy You showed on the cross, Lord Jesus, for volunteering to suffer for us— unthinkable!—and that You have been patient with us. We blindly carry on in our lives. But You paid for it.

We exalt You, Lord Jesus, exalt the work of the cross, exalt Your love, O heavenly Father. We honor You, O Holy Spirit. Lord, cleanse us, purify us, keep our eyes off ourselves and on You. Let the readers of this book fall in love with You, O God Almighty: Father, Son, and Holy Spirit. Let their lives be blessed beyond imagination. We pray they might stay close to You and not allow the flesh, the world, or the devil to destroy your work.

We believe that You will do what we have requested for Your glory.

We commit these words to You with joy, Lord, joy from the heart.

In the name of Jesus,
Amen.

CHAPTER 1

Seek First the Kingdom

My Mother, Matilde Balfour de Palau

Seek first his kingdom and his righteousness,
and all these things will be given to you as well.

MATTHEW 6:33

I was born in Argentina, in a humble town full of proud people. Ingeniero Maschwitz is its name. In its day, "Maschwitz" was classy, a weekend home for people eager to get out of the stifling capital city. But time has not been kind to the little town. Gradually, the buildings' paint has faded and peeled, and the weekend visitors stopped coming out so often. Back then, Buenos Aires was forty-five minutes away . . . and seemed farther.

There was a paved highway between us and the big city, but the streets I played on were mostly dirt, shaded from the hot sun by wide-spreading trees. I learned to know what time it was by the noises and whistles of the train, which was only a few blocks from our home, even though as a child it seemed miles away.

I was the firstborn to my parents, the only boy of six children. Our home life was very happy, full of laughter and the smell of good food, coffee, and *mate*, the hot green tea that Argentines love to sip through *bombillas*—silver straws with a strainer at the far end. (I never cared for *mate*.)

My parents set the foundation for my life. They did this in many ways, but none were more important than their heartfelt and unwavering commitment to the Gospel. For Luis and Matilde Palau, the Good News of Jesus was something to be preached *and* lived, proclaimed on the street corners *and* demonstrated by love at home.

I am starting with my mom because she was with us children longer. The greatest lesson I learned from my mother was a complete trust in God, even amid radically changing and unpleasant circumstances. Her trust and joy in the Lord was like a "house built upon the rock." When the storms and floods came, they were not cast down.

But more on those storms later. My life was warm and happy as a young child. When I was born, we were well off. By the standards of that day, we were not extravagantly rich, or even ritzy by today's American upper-middle-class standards, but my father had done very well for us.

Our family had a maid who cleaned and helped with the cooking, nannies for the children, and a driver for my mother, as she did not drive. We lived comfortably and happy. I remember warm Christmases, which we celebrated in the European style, complete with a trimmed evergreen tree. My dad always surprised us. Candies and treats abounded. One year I was given a bicycle— quite a gift! Another time I received a pony, complete with a sharp cowboy outfit for the new *gaucho* in the Palau family. The pony soon died, however. And what a fuss I made! I'm afraid I was a bit of a pain.

Other than school and my father's business, our life was completely centered on church, worship, evangelism, and work. Most of our neighbors in the town saw us as symbols of evangelical faith, which in that day was not welcomed by many of our nominally Roman Catholic neighbors.

There is a photo of me, long haired and diapered—two years old, perhaps—peering through the slats of our fence at a religious procession stopped in the street in front of our house. The more devout folks of the town would hold a yearly parade for the feast day of the Virgin of Luján. Today, Catholics think of us evangelicals more fondly—as "separated brethren"—but that day they made a point of halting for ten or fifteen minutes in front of the Palau residence, carrying a statue of the Virgin Mary in triangular robes of blue and white, her gentle face peeping out from beneath a golden crown. By the time they got to us, they had carried the image all over town, singing a slowly rolling dirge-like hymn:

O Maria, Madre mia,
O consuelo del mortal.

They meant well, but to my little ears it sounded like a dead hymn. As I grew older, I wanted to call out to them, "Come on, don't you have any happier songs than that?"

The Palau family had not always been on that side of the fence. Only a few years earlier, my mother had been the organist for the Roman Catholic parish church. Perhaps that is why the more traditional religious people of our little town made a point of stopping.

My mother's father was Scotch Presbyterian and constantly referred to himself as one. "Don't worry about me, sonny," he'd say smugly if a missionary approached him. "I'm all right—Scotch

Presbyterian!" In his mind, that ended the conversation. (I have often remarked to my friends that he liked the Scotch better than the Presbyterian.)

Though my grandfather's faith appeared nominal, my mother's mother was devout in a way I suspect only French Catholic grandmothers can be. She was decidedly *not* Scotch Presbyterian. My grandmother once promised the Virgin to walk on her knees for three kilometers on the Virgin's feast day if Mary kept my uncle Jackie from being pressed into military service. Ridiculous, you know? But she did it, and she bled. But she fulfilled her promise. In later years she came to know the Lord more fully. "I doubt the Virgin Mary even heard me!" she commented later.

Like my grandmother, my mother's faith was heartfelt. But it failed to bring her peace and left her seeking something more. By the time she was pregnant with me, she was experiencing a quiet crisis.

One day a polite knock sounded at the front door, and as the Lord would have it, my mother was home to answer it. How I praise God for that! On the step was a sharply dressed British man with a fine-looking book in one hand and a heavy walking stick in the other. "*Buenos Dias, Senora,*" he said. "Would you like a copy of the Word of God?"

I do not know if my mother had ever owned a Bible, but she took the one that the British gentleman handed her, thanked him politely, and closed the door. She looked at the book, a very nice copy of the New Testament in Spanish. She began to read. The feelings that were pent up for so long began to overwhelm her. She had been unable to find what her soul craved—*peace*. She had done good works and served in church. She had made promises to

God. She was a faithful worshiper at Mass. She confessed regularly to her priest. And yet, despite it all, something was still missing. She did not have peace.

There is an old Spanish hymn that brings me to tears even today as I sit nearly seven thousand miles from the old house in Maschwitz. My voice cannot finish it without breaking. In English, it runs like this:

> *Peace with God, I tried to find it*
> *With feverish desire.*
> *But my meritorious work*
> *Did not give me health.*
> *O, what peace*
> *The Lord gives us!*

That so perfectly sums up my mother's search. She began to read the New Testament the man had given her. So deep was her reverence for Jesus, even in her searching, that she read it on her knees, knowing it to be holy. After only a few chapters in the Gospel of Matthew, she came to the Beatitudes, that most famous sermon of Jesus that begins in Matthew 5.

"*Bienaventurados*," she read, "*los de limpio corazón: porque ellos verán á Dios.*"

"Blessed are the pure in heart: for they shall see God."

She read this verse of blessing, full of beauty from the mouth of Jesus. She read it and despaired. It was as if the book was speaking to her. *That's it*, she thought, *I will never see God. I know that I do not have a pure heart.*

But as she was praying, she felt something strange. She felt that the Lord who had said those words was speaking to her. *My daughter*, she felt Him speak inside, *you are mine. You are forgiven.* She suddenly remembered the words of John the Baptist that the priest would quote at the Mass: "Behold, the Lamb of God who takes away the sin of the world." She knew, in a sudden flood of joy, that this Lamb was for *her*! She saw Him! He had come to take the sin of Matilde!

She put it all together for the first time there on her knees. She wept, she told me later, as the Holy Spirit moved her. The lack of peace, the sense of overwhelming impurity in her heart— they should not lead her to despair! They should point her to the Lamb! Her fears—*I will never find peace with God, and I will never be forgiven*—were overcome by that simple reminder: *Behold the Lamb of God. . . . Behold the Lamb of God.*

And she felt peace and joy and love. Finally, she found rest, the very thing she had so feverishly desired.

Overjoyed, my mother went to find the well-dressed man who'd given her the New Testament. His name was Mr. Edward Charles Rogers. She asked him if she should leave the Catholic church. "No, no! Stay there," he urged. "Keep playing the organ for them. Tell your friends what you've experienced. Tell them how the Lord has brought peace to your heart. Many of them are probably still searching for what you have found. Then, in the evenings, come join our Bible meetings in our little chapel." And that is what she did.

I was in her womb when she was converted. Before I was born, she prayed, *Lord, I want him to be a preacher of the Gospel.* And that seems to have worked out! She told many stories like this as I grew up, which reinforced in me the feeling that first came in boyhood— before I fully knew what it meant to be a Christian! *Luis,* I felt inside, *you've been called to preach the Gospel. You'd better do it!*

This prayer of hers, even as such a young believer, shows the pure sincerity of her seeking. The same quiet commitment that made her search for inner peace, even though all the trappings of outward religion had been hers, now motivated her to a constant, deep spiritual life that overflowed for her husband, children, and neighbors.

My mom almost loved me to excess! Life was great. I felt like a good boy. Mom enthusiastically applauded everything her children did. I remember learning to read and her ringing praise: "Oh! So young, and he can read so well!" On and on. Perhaps it spoiled me a bit, but I had no doubt how much she loved me.

My mother centered her life on God: Father, Son, and Holy Spirit. I can hear her voice still, hushing in prayer, rising in praise. She read the Bible constantly, almost always on her knees like she had from the beginning. She quoted many verses to us from memory, and she insisted that we memorize the verses we were given in Sunday school.

She emphasized Scripture memorization for children. For me, helping children learn and memorize the Word is a big deal, and that comes straight from my mom. Our Sunday school would give us little prizes for memorizing the weekly verses. The class would repeat the verse together, and if someone didn't know it, the class would help them out. It was fun, and we were so proud when we learned the passages. The promises of those verses stuck with me. Back then, they were powerful. Today, those verses have the strength of promises fulfilled.

Of the many verses that my mother loved, one sums up perfectly the lesson that she taught me: "Seek first his kingdom and his righteousness, and all these things will be given to you as well" (Matthew 6:33).

What a simple promise. But how profound! All the things we worry about—what we will eat, drink, and wear—will be supplied by God as we seek His kingdom. It is an audacious promise that Jesus made. Like the surrounding verses in Matthew 6 ask, my mother trusted God innocently and completely, like the birds of the air or the lilies of the field. Little did she know how much that trust would be tested.

My father died when he was only thirty-four. I was ten. When Dad passed, he left no paperwork: no will, no estate plan, no paper trail for much of his property, and no real organization of his business interests, which were considerable and complicated.

Dad was primarily a builder, but he had his hand in just about everything you can imagine—even today we don't really know how much property he owned or the full extent of his business interests. In fact, the week he returned home and died, he'd been up north in central Argentina at a province called Mendoza where he had purchased some vineyards. We found out about the vineyards twenty years later. By that time it was too late—someone had paid the back taxes and taken them over. He owned a lot of land, equipment, and materials, but we simply couldn't find proper records for them. He was a busy young man, always building, always on to the next thing.

My mom, who knew nothing about business, was left to fend for herself. There she was, thirty-three and expecting my youngest sister, with six children and widowed. She tried to settle my dad's accounts but could do little in her state of grief and shock to counteract the people who were demanding money or making claims to the Palau company. It was a terrible time for her. In only a matter of months, our family went from well-off to essentially destitute.

People hounded us, saying we owed them money. It became so bad that we had to leave Maschwitz. It was a heart-wrenching time for my mother. We had no source of income. "I don't know what to do," she'd say. "The Lord has to protect us. He has to provide."

My mom was quite staunch about not taking people to court. She decided not to sue anybody and let God do the suing. "He will provide," she repeated again and again.

She felt the pain of loneliness. Not long after my father's death, when I was eleven or twelve, we were staying in my grandfather's house on the other side of Buenos Aires. I remember my mother retreating to a bedroom. Soon I heard her crying. In Argentina, everyone drinks wine, just like Europeans—there is no stigma about it for Christians. She had taken a glass of wine and some bread and cheese and was sobbing over them in the bedroom. I realized that she was weeping because my father was not there with her. At first I thought, *She's missing my dad. But she has us!* But later I thought, *Maybe that's why she is crying. Six of us to deal with, and now she is poor. I'd cry too!* But she remained strong.

Six years after Dad died, we had to move to Córdoba, in central Argentina, four hundred miles from the beautiful home my father had built. I had to leave the private British education that had been my father's heartfelt wish for me. My present and future shifted. Córdoba was hilly and beautiful, but the city was large, and life was very different.

You've heard of downsizing? Oh, did we downsize! Our new place had a garage, but we did not have a car, so the garage became my sisters' bedroom. Since I was the only boy, I slept in the tiny living room on a bed that doubled as a couch. We were poor. Very poor.

Even that little place, so cramped with the seven of us, was too expensive. At one point we were nine months behind on our rent. We simply couldn't pay. But during the hardship, people around us extended small graces—the landlord looked the other way until we could pay what we owed. The man at the corner grocer allowed us credit, even though the Palau family's bills grew and grew.

Occasionally a little money would come in, and my mother

would go and pay people what they were owed. And they let us do that. As far as I know, these were not believers—they simply were people being kind to a widow and her six kids. Their kindness has always touched me. The kindness of unbelievers can be the provision of God.

Years passed and I grew. I landed a job as an employee at the Bank of London in South America. My salary was good, comparatively, but it was still a kid's salary, and I had five sisters and a mother, besides myself, to support! Even though I worked full-time, we simply did not have enough money. Because we were bilingual, people often thought we were upper-class, despite our deep poverty. The people in the local church, most of whom were very humble, always assumed that we were wealthy. I worked for the Bank of London after all! As a result, I think people were unaware of our true needs. Although the people from our new church in Córdoba were generous by nature, no one said, "Madame, you're a widow with six children. Here's a check." So we depended fully on the Lord.

We had absolutely *nothing*. Sometimes we had a cup of coffee and one loaf of French bread, torn into seven parts. That's it. Yet we would get on our knees and thank the Lord for the coffee and the bread. Occasionally, Mom would scrape enough money together to buy a single steak. One steak cut neatly into seven little bits, one for each of us. Despite the immense difficulty, I think it was a blessing to be poor. It helped me understand the poor. I truly know what it feels like not to have enough.

Yet I do not remember my mother complaining or expressing anger at what God had allowed our life to become. She proved that her trust was not conditional. Even when circumstances had changed so drastically, she never stopped seeking God's kingdom. We trusted the Lord because there was no one else to trust.

Trusting the Lord during a storm—that is trust. Faith like that makes an impression on those around you. Trust is easy in the bright times of life. But the true test of belief comes in the darkness of adversity. Our family would kneel together, and my mother would lead us in a prayer for God's provision. Always looking to the Lord, always depending on the Lord, we had nowhere else to turn. Though life was difficult, not once did He fail us.

She often quoted Scripture: "Trust in the Lord with all your heart" (Proverbs 3:5), and "My God shall supply all your need according to his riches in glory by Christ Jesus" (Philippians 4:19 KJV).

The simple faith that sprung from those verses moved her to sing. She was a terrible singer! But she still was always singing. Our house was filled with the sound of her voice, often with my sisters happily joining in. I remember hearing her sing behind the house as she did the laundry that a maid once did for her. It still stirs me to tears remembering it. She sang all sorts of songs, usually in Spanish. The one I remember most fondly was a familiar hymn:

> *And can it be that I should gain*
> *An interest in the Savior's blood?*
> *Died he for me, who caused his pain—*
> *For me, who him to death pursued?*
> *Amazing love! How can it be,*
> *That thou, my God, shouldst die for me?*

God's provision came in a variety of ways, as it usually does. We worked hard, we received the generosity of others, and there were plenty of surprises.

My mother was always an avid reader, constantly reading us the biographies of great missionaries and Christian workers. She often read them in English because in those days few Christian books were in Spanish. My first memory of her reading these stories is when I was about four years old. The one that struck me most deeply was about Hudson Taylor and his remarkable mission to China. Those men and women missionaries were my heroes, and they still are. Basketball players and musicians are not my heroes; they're just gifted millionaires. Those who give their lives for the service of others, those who put their own comfort or safety aside to bring the Good News of Jesus to people who have never heard— they are the real heroes.

Because my mom was bilingual, she was able to translate books for the Salvation Army and other Christian organizations to earn a little money. She also picked up jobs for corporations needing translation. Her work sure helped, but it didn't pay enough to change our situation.

Our family stepped in when they could. We had an aunt—my mother's sister—who was gracious and generous. She never had children and worked for a British college in a good position as assistant to the principal. She bought my sisters dresses and sent a little money on our birthdays. She and her husband were not wealthy, but they shared what they had.

I laugh as I think back—that uncle, before he was married to my aunt, carried a .45-caliber pistol. There weren't many streetlights in those days. If he heard a noise in the darkness behind the house, he'd throw a window open and—*bang bang bang*—start shooting in the air. "What are you doing over there!" he'd shout out at nothing. *Bang bang bang!* What a terrible sense of public safety! He could have killed someone! Even though he was only nineteen, he had to act the man, you know?

Eventually, my sister Matilde went to work for Kaiser, an American company that made cars for the postwar market. They had a factory in Argentina, and bilingual people were in high demand.

My sister Martha was very talented. She taught piano and

accordion lessons for children, anything musical to earn a few dollars.

We learned to live with almost nothing and yet be used by the Lord. While we were receiving help from others, we worked to help others too. On Saturdays, we visited two very poor French sisters, who were practically shut-ins. Our visits were a ministry. We brought them food, sang, and preached Bible messages (good practice for later).

When one of the sisters died, we begged for a cheap coffin from the local municipality. As we gathered to remember her and offer our condolences, the remaining sister pulled me aside. "Luis," she said, "in France we worry that we might bury someone when they aren't really dead. So . . ." She showed me an old-fashioned hatpin, long and sharp. ". . . we take one of these and push it into the sole of their foot." I shuddered. "If they're alive, they'll kick."

I stared.

"I don't dare do it," she continued. "Would you do the honor for my sister?"

I took the hatpin and went to the body. Though I hesitated, the pin didn't. It slipped in with horrible smoothness, as if the flesh were butter. Ack! It was awful. But we knew she was dead, and her sister had peace of mind. It was an early introduction to the strange requests that ministering for Jesus makes of us.

We ministered as best we could in the hills of Córdoba, a city of about a million. We held children's meetings in our house and in the open air. We held street meetings. We would do anything to proclaim the Gospel. Sharing it was our life. Sports, movies, all that stuff—*pfft*. We spoke of everything other than witnessing and missionary work as the "world" back then, and we despised it. We just preached the Gospel.

I bought a little motorbike to commute to my job at the bank and my job at a missions organization, first called Orient Mission, later Overseas Crusades. The new job paid a *little* bit better, but it sure wasn't the big-time.

Besides school, odd jobs, and work, all that we did was go to church. On Tuesday we went for Bible study, Thursday for preaching, Saturday for *something*, and Sunday for Sunday school, more preaching, and communion. Church and street witnessing were our life.

Once, a dear friend told me that God answers prayers four ways:

1. Yes, I thought you'd never ask.
2. No, I love you too much.
3. Yes, but not yet.
4. Yes, and here's more.

I added a fifth, from personal experience:

5. Yes, but not the way you think.

God answers prayer. Always. But He answers in His way, not ours. We must listen for the nuance of His answer. He is not bound by our plans or desires.

The years after Dad died taught us that fifth point. God's answers meant hard work or credit from neighbors. Occasionally, something remarkable would happen.

The Bible talks about cheating widows and orphans. We experienced it. One month when money was tighter than normal, we were expecting to *finally* be thrown out of our house because we were behind several months on our rent. Just as our financial situation was becoming a crisis, a letter came.

"Mrs. Palau," it began in simple, masculine handwriting, "I am embarrassed to tell this to you. Years ago, when you were in trouble, I lied to you. I took a tractor that I said was broken. In fact, it worked perfectly well. I have used it for years, and am ashamed that I did this to you, a widow—with six children!"

It was signed with the name of an old acquaintance. In the envelope was a check for a significant amount, as much as the man calculated that he owed my mother for having cheated her out of an expensive tractor—plus interest. We were able to stay in our home!

That letter highlighted the fact that there was still much my father left behind that was rightfully ours. Eventually, after struggling for years with the government and lawyers and unscrupulous people who had been close to our family and had, speaking frankly, cheated us shamelessly, we got a fraction of it back.

When I was thirty-two, twenty-two years after Dad's death, we discovered properties that were still in the family name. Eventually the ownership, through all the legal ramifications of a messy inheritance like that, came to us. Under Argentine law, 50 percent went to my mom, and the remainder was divided among his six children. It wasn't much, but it felt awfully good.

At that point, I had seen and experienced so many people plagued by greed that I was nearly sickened by the thought of money for myself. I thought, *I don't want a penny of this.* Knowing I would be able to provide for myself more easily than my sisters, I added my percentage to my oldest sister's so that she could have a little property as a safety net. I didn't feel like a hero for doing that. I just felt glad. I felt happy and at peace.

With the newly increased financial stability, my mother paid off her debts. At some point—I don't remember precisely when— our family was able to say, "We don't owe money to anyone." The Lord had answered our prayers but in unexpected ways and in His time.

From the time I was kicking in the womb, my mother prayed I would preach the Gospel. "Go to towns that don't have a church!" she'd urge me. "Take the Gospel. Plant churches." She pushed and encouraged: "Go, go, go."

For my mother, seeking God's kingdom wasn't something you just did on your knees; it was something you did on your feet. She was constantly pushing me to preach. I held back a bit at first. I was young and felt the responsibility of the family on my shoulders. After a while, she wanted me to leave my job at the bank to go preach the Gospel. "But Mom," I'd say, "how are we going to eat?"

"The Lord will provide," she'd reply. "He's no man's debtor."

But it took me a while to take that step of faith. I didn't act as quickly as she hoped I would. Once my mother and I were walking out in the hills of Córdoba. "You have to get over there," she said, pointing to the horizon. "You have to go preach. You need to go plant a church." Her words brought up something I'd been struggling with. I knew that I *ought* to consider full-time ministry, but I had been putting it off. But I never felt the emotional pull of a call from God to go.

"Mom, I'm waiting for the call," I said.

"The call?" she said, with that dry tone only a mother perfects. "The *call!*" She was getting upset. "The call went out two thousand years ago, Luis! The Lord's waiting for *your* answer; you're not waiting for *His* call."

She made a good point. Who says we have to wait for God's call? If He calls us in a special way, fine. But He has ordered us to go. We don't need a call. We just need to obey. An absent "call" was never supposed to become an excuse for inaction. My mom was never "called." Her Bible simply told her to "go." And so deeply did she take that calling to heart that she spent her life obeying it with joy and teaching her children to do the same.

That conversation shook me up. It was one of the defining moments of my life. I decided that I was done waiting around for a feeling that might never come, and I would simply obey what had been in front of me the whole time. I didn't need to wait. I needed to *do.*

As we sought the kingdom, following my mother's example, we saw God provide—and even provide through us! Yes, "all these things shall be added unto you" (Matthew 6:33 KJV). Although those times were difficult, God provided.

Experiencing God's provision taught me to trust in His uncommon methods. Through the unwavering example of my dear mother, I have seen that God is trustworthy. Although my faith has been tested many times over the seven decades since my father died, God has never proved faithless to his promise.

We were not thinking consciously of it then. We just sought Him and His kingdom. Looking back, I see that our poverty helped teach us how to see ourselves as part of an invisible economy, the system of the kingdom of heaven. By God's grace, this system can supply our every need with elegant timing and by the simple miracles that God uses so often.

All the Palau children are serving the Lord in our own way. We all have our ups and downs, but we have all worked for the kingdom. When my sisters write to me, they often mention the trust we learned from my mother. "We've trusted Him from the beginning," they say. They are right. The Lord has answered our prayers. We have seen His provision through thick and thin. He has supplied a lifetime's worth of our needs. Perfectly.

My mother lived to see the answer to her prayer. I became a preacher, and I traveled the world over, sharing the simple Good News of the cross. Whenever I would return from a trip, I'd call her up. She always wanted to know about how the ministry went. She prayed for me relentlessly. She sought the kingdom until the day she passed on to her reward in heaven. She was faithful to the end and died singing in that voice of hers, a happy, firm believer.

I learned so much from my mother. Foremost among those riches was a solid-rock trust in God and his promises. Her faith proved to be immovable. "In this world you will have trouble. But take heart! I have overcome the world" (John 16:33). She believed that, sang that, taught that, prayed that, hoped that, laughed, cried, and lived that.

These days, I've been thinking a lot about the cross. My cancer has put the fire under me—as if it wasn't there already! It has made me a holy *fiend* upon the subject of the cross. The cross of Jesus has been the center of everything. It *must* be the center of everything. It must be the center of my life. It must be the center of yours. I must see myself in the light of the cross and remember I am nothing without Jesus.

And neither are you, whoever is reading this. We all face the grave. Let's not kid ourselves. We talk about it throughout life. For me, though, death has always seemed distant. It doesn't anymore. I think of the gaping dark hole that death could have been for me. But that grave has been swallowed up in victory. Its sting broken. Why? Because of Jesus Christ!

Great revivals come when the cross of Jesus is preached. The cross puts everything in focus. His cross is the center of everything that's good in the world. The preaching of that cross was a mission that consumed my mother's heart. She had every excuse to stay at home and just try to manage. She was a widow living in a house with seven mouths to feed! But she used the simplicity of our lives as another way to seek the kingdom and always worked to share the Gospel with as many people as possible.

From Matthew 6:33 I got the concept of seeking the kingdom first, and I believe it today. God has promised that He will provide for what you need. He does not promise riches, prosperity, or comfort, but He will give you what you need to move forward in the work and life of His good kingdom. The Lord's promises are many; I cannot deny them.

What are your needs? How are you seeking the Lord's kingdom today? Are you in need of provision that only your Creator and Redeemer can give? Have you ever tasted the goodness of the Lord's perfect provision?

I want you to remember the example of my mother. Such simple faith she had—that God's promise stood *for her*. She believed that as she sought the kingdom, God would respond as He promised to faithfully give what she needed.

My prayer for you, dear reader, is the same one I am praying for myself. I pray that we may always turn to the Lord for every need we have, small or great. I pray that we might be found loyal in seeking the Lord daily so that we might experience the richness of his provision with the same depth of faith that I saw in my mother, Matilde Balfour de Palau.

CHAPTER 2

Give Everything to God

My Father, Luis Palau Sr.

You will be enriched in every way so that
you can be generous on every occasion,
and through us your generosity will result in
thanksgiving to God.

2 CORINTHIANS 9:11

When I was a boy, the lady who lived across the street acciden-tally electrocuted herself.

I watched her grab that fateful wire. She began shaking like a fish on the line. Her screams brought the neighborhood running, but it was my father who acted.

Like Britain, Argentina uses 220-volt wiring, twice as strong as the 110-volt residential wiring in the United States. It is furiously powerful. But my father did not hesitate for a moment. Running across the street, he grabbed a nearby two-by-four and swung like a baseball player making a line drive. He struck her arm, breaking the current and undoubtedly saving her life. The whole town heard about it and praised him as a hero. To me, he had always been.

His impulse to act while others watched—putting his life on the line—was characteristic of his whole life. In business, in sports (soccer), in church ministry, in family, he was a man who fully committed. He did not waffle or waver. He saw what needed to be done and did it.

That full commitment was a kind of generosity. His giving was not limited to his money or time. He gave *himself* to those around him.

Dad was pure east-coast Spanish. He was from L'Escala, a little coastal town in Catalonia. His family sensed the growing violence and fascism in Spain after World War I. There were bombings and all sorts of trouble with the central government in Madrid. War was in the air again. Many Spaniards sought a fresh start in the Americas. In about 1922, my father's family moved to Argentina.

Dad came from a large family with two sisters and four brothers. Seven kids total. He was the second oldest, and the clear leader of the family, My dad began supporting his family at sixteen when his own father died. His mother, my grandmother, lived nearby when I was young. She owned a little shop with candy and conveniences. She and two of my aunts attended our church. My parents were married at the Catholic church in Escobar, a little town near ours.

Although my father was a quiet man, he was very warm and loving. He showed his affection, kissing and hugging us like the good Latin he was. He was constantly bringing little gifts and treats for his wife and kids, giving us little reminders that he was thinking about us and wanted to see us smile.

I was mischievous and perhaps just the slightest bit overindulged. Once, I cut my sister's hair as if I were her barber. I have to say, I did a pretty good job for being so young. Sadly, I was the only one who appreciated my work. So I decided against a career in hairdressing and laid low for a while.

One day, I hid from Dad (we called him Papito) behind a woodpile with my sister. "Luisito! Where are you?" he called. "Where are you?" Finally, we started giggling so much that he found us. That day, I learned a lesson about hiding for play when your parents are calling you for real.

Dad had a small farm—perhaps the size of two city blocks—that was managed by employees. They grew corn, kept a small herd of cattle, and raised chickens. They farmed in the small, old-fashioned way that the world needs to reclaim. I remember happily crunching on the corn and drinking fresh milk from the cows. I remember racing my sisters to collect eggs from the chickens, trying not to break their shells in our eager fingers.

My father was a very capable gardener—his hard work and quiet patience suited him well for growing things. A gardener knows he cannot rush nature, and so his work ethic takes on an attentive, watchful quality that moves at the natural pace of life.

Dad gave me a section of ground behind our home to plant my own garden. "This is yours, Luis," he said to me. "Take care of it." He taught me to plant tomatoes, lettuce, and climbing vines like beans and peas. I proudly tended my little plot. I was only nine, but I wanted to make my father proud. There, in the garden, he let me know that gardening was only the beginning of his training to help me grow into a self-sufficient man. "When you turn sixteen, I'll buy you a little pickup truck," he said. "Then you can begin to work for yourself."

Working for myself would have been following in his footsteps. As a teenager with an old pickup, Dad began his career delivering building supplies. It wasn't long before he was the one doing the building. His business principles were simple—work hard, be honest, and build with unpretentious quality. My dad owned about four city blocks of empty fields. Slowly he developed them, building homes to sell.

My father's office ran the company from our house, a beautiful home that he'd remodeled extensively. Sometimes, when he was trying to work, I would gather him, my sisters, and any of their friends unfortunate enough to be around and preach at them. Dad took weekends off but worked what they called "*sábado inglés*," an "English Saturday," a half day. So he was free on Saturday afternoons and all day Sunday, plus holidays. And during the week in the summer, he took time off whenever he wanted.

His building style was strong and practical, but it was pretty too. He favored the European chalet style. He built with a lot of brick and put all the amenities indoors, which was a big deal in the days of outdoor plumbing and outhouses. I wish I had more information about what he built during his career, but sadly, I don't. As a grown man, I visited one house he built and was deeply impressed. It was beautiful, sturdy, and obviously made with skill and care.

My mother's and father's conversions were separated by about a year. I was in my mother's womb when she met Jesus and an infant when my dad did.

After my twenty-two-year-old mother came to know the Lord, she wanted her husband to have the same peace and joy that she had found. She tried to share with my father, but he had little interest. He didn't fight her about it, but he made it clear that he was not interested.

My father played soccer in his spare time. He was a tough,

muscled athlete in addition to his business skill and industry as an entrepreneur. I have a photo of him with his team, taken on one of the Sunday mornings when they used to play. He has a stern expression (though you can see a little playfulness around the eyes), and he's holding flowers from a recent team victory.

Add to that natural masculinity—which should not oppose Christianity but often tries to—the influence of Latin culture, which thinks of religion as the domain of women, children, and the elderly. Faith was not *macho* for Argentine men in their prime. It was a crutch, something to comfort the fearful and the weak. Of course, nothing could be further from the truth. But my father had to learn that for himself.

Eventually, my mother felt her duty to the parish was done, and she decided to go to the Plymouth Brethren church. She was rebaptized by immersion—a significant step in that culture.

My father drove her faithfully to church every Sunday. He would drop her off, as most Latin men would, then go for a drink with his buddies and return when the service was over. But one Sunday night, he parked instead of pulling away, and to my mother's surprise, he came into the chapel with her.

In the middle of the service, while the preaching was in full swing, he suddenly stood up and announced, "I receive Jesus Christ as my only and sufficient Savior." And he sat down. It was that simple.

My dad did nothing halfway. As Mr. Edward Charles Rogers said about my father, "The day Luis Palau was converted, his wallet was converted as well." Dad lived his faith through a totally generous commitment of his heart, energy, thought, time, and yes, money. After his conversion, he was relentless in both evangelism and generosity. He would build homes for needy people, hand them the title, shake their hand, and say, "Pay me as much as you can per month." That looseness with the details (in service of others) came back to bite our family when he died, as there were few records of what he'd done with a simple handshake agreement or a slap on the back. But there was a generous heart behind it.

Spanish and English have a funny relationship for me. I think in both languages, write in both languages, preach in both languages. It can get confusing. I often catch myself about to use a word from the other language. It can be frustrating because sometimes one language has the *perfect* phrase, but I can't use it in the other! In Latin America, I forget English. I think exclusively in Spanish. When we come back to the United States, Spanish takes the backseat. I even take a different Bible depending on which language I'll be using.

My father didn't speak English, but Mom did. We spoke Spanish in the home growing up, but we kids were bilingual because of Mom. Still, with an eye to my future, Dad sent me to a British boarding school in Quilmes to refine my English and give me the best education available.

I went to the local public schools until I was eight. (In public school I was once forced to kneel on dried corn because I refused to pray to the Virgin.) Then I began at a private school that I commuted to daily by train. A private school like that was a privilege, but I was too young to appreciate it.

A rather humorous moment prompted my parents to move me from the private school to boarding school at the prestigious and disciplined Quilmes Prep School. One school day, my mother and father received a phone call from an administrator at my school. My parents had assumed that I was studiously learning at my private day school. "Where is Luis?" the administrator asked. "Is he alright?" My parents didn't know. I had left on time. The administrator assured them that I never showed up.

Can you imagine my parents' response? I was missing! They went straight to the train station. "Oh yes, I've seen him," the station master said in response to their flurry of questions. "Wait here a little while and you will too. He's just coming and going on the trains. He gets off one and hops on another. Over and over again, all morning long, just looking out of the windows."

Soon they caught me. My father announced later that if I was going to play games, I could play them at boarding school. "This isn't a punishment," Dad said clearly after calling me into his office. "I wanted to send you anyway. I want you to learn good English. It's the language of the future." So I was off to Quilmes Prep School.

The day Dad died, he had just purchased two ships. They were full of sand from Paraguay. He planned on using the sand for some of his building projects and selling the excess to local companies that made brick and cement. Whatever the details of that transaction were, he never completed the deal.

He was working over a holiday weekend when he caught the pneumonia that eventually killed him. He was helping his workers unload construction materials. He was young and strong, unconcerned by the cough that slowly took hold of his chest. Whatever it was, he'd beat it easily. At least that's how he brushed off my mother's growing concerns about his cough.

But he didn't beat it. By the time he got to the hospital, it was too late. The doctors said that they might have been able to save him if he'd come in immediately. But the war had left the country terribly short on penicillin, and there was nothing they could do. He returned home after the doctors gave up hope. It was all so sudden. My grandmother called, then picked me up from school in Quilmes, and put me on the train home to Maschwitz.

For the entire trip home, I felt in my heart that I was too late. I just knew.

It was December 17, 1944, the height of summer in the southern hemisphere. I ran off the train and through town, sweating in the oppressive heat. Bursting through the door at home, I knew immediately that he had already died. The hush over the house was unmistakable. It wasn't a hush of anticipation. It was a hush of acceptance.

I ran into his room, surprising my relatives, who halfheartedly tried to slow me down. My mother was weeping. She was being comforted by various family members, who bustled about in silence, doing everything one does when there's nothing else that can be done.

I knew why they tried to restrain me when I reached my father's room. Was this the man who laughed as he tossed me in the air? Was this the man whose knelt on his hands and knees in the dirt to teach me how to plant tomatoes? He had been so strong and healthy.

Now, his body was horribly discolored, yellow, and dehydrated. His lips were cracked. The summer heat was beginning to take its toll. Death had taken Dad.

No words can describe my mourning.

My mother, pregnant with my youngest sister, Ruth, told me about his passing. He knew he was dying when he left the hospital. A couple hours before his death, he sat up in bed and sang a familiar hymn about heaven: "Bright crowns up there, bright crowns for you and me."

When the song was over, he fell back on the pillow, pointed upward, and quoted Paul's words in Philippians: "I'm going to be with Jesus, 'which is better by far.'" These were his last words.

When I asked why they hadn't called me earlier, my family told me, "It all just happened so fast."

There was no part of our family's life that his death did not affect. Mother, me, Matilde, Martha, Ketty, Margarita, and even our family dog—who curled up by the door and would not eat for days—knew that our lives would simply never be the same.

As was the custom, we stayed up all night with our relatives and friends, preparing for his burial the next day. In those days, they always had an open casket. Because of the heat, they filled the room where his body lay with thick bouquets of flowers. To this day I cannot stand the heavy, overpowering scent of flowers. They make me sick. Easter lilies are the worst because our house was packed with them. For many they symbolize resurrection. To me they smell of death and mourning. I tried so hard to stay awake, watching the body with my mother, but eventually I fell asleep.

The next day, one of the missionaries did the service since Mr. Rogers was out of town. The missionary reminded us of Christ's statement: "I am the resurrection and the life" (John 11:25).

I catch myself humming a hymn we sang at the funeral from time to time, even today, knowing that my own death is not so far away:

> *Face to face with Christ my Savior,*
> *Face to face—what will it be,*
> *When with rapture I behold Him,*
> *Jesus Christ, who died for me?*
> *What rejoicing in His presence,*
> *When are banished grief and pain;*
> *When the crooked ways are straightened*
> *And the dark things shall be plain.*

It might be easy to sing about, but these dark things didn't seem like they could ever be made plain.

Two of my aunts took care of all the children. Though I was

there beside the casket in our home, my aunts didn't want me to go to the cemetery. They felt it would be traumatic to see my dad put in the ground. But I created a distraction and escaped out the window. I ran to one of the trucks, greeted one of my father's laborers, and pleaded, "Don't tell anyone. Let me hide here. I am going to the cemetery."

He helped me, and I went. I wanted to be the first one to throw a clod of dirt on my father's coffin. And, darting through the legs of some of the men surrounding the grave, surprising the whole assembly, I was.

Though my father was a quiet man, he was not shy, and he was public in his faith. Like his first confession, standing up in the middle of a sermon to announce his belief, no social convention or inner fear could control his tongue when he felt deeply about something. But even to those close to him, he was rather private. For years after he died, my sisters and I asked our mother to tell us more about him. She quickly ran out of stories. Though there must have been much about his life to tell, she did not know it. In those days, strong men were like that, quiet and self-contained, with their actions speaking words their mouths would never say.

My father included his family in his work and ministry. Our family traveled together in my father's small fleet of trucks to nearby towns to hold street meetings. My sisters and I would ride on my dad's truck, with *Palau* painted boldly on the side for his construction business. We would stand around to form a little audience. After all, no one likes to be the first person to stop and listen to a street preacher.

We would haul a pump organ along for my mother to play and sing. Oh, what an awful sound! The reedy tones of the organ rose up with a whine, and my mother sang with more enthusiasm than pitch. But her heart was gifted, and the pure faith she sang with had a beauty of its own. And people came. They stopped. They were converted.

My dad preached regularly in church. His favorite passage was Psalm 95:6–7: "O come, let us worship and bow down: let us kneel before the LORD our maker. For he is our God; and we are the people of his pasture, and the sheep of his hand" (KJV).

The whole town knew about his conversion. He was a respected man with some social status, so his conversion made an impact. The stories of his generosity seem unending. He was kind to the poor and weak to the detriment of his organization and finances. Knowing him to be so openhanded, people took advantage.

My father's generous spirit extended to every aspect of his life. If it was his, it was his to give away. He truly gave everything to God, not simply his money. He gave his time, his skill as a builder, his macho reputation, and he took on a role with the often-mocked Brethren church. He blessed people with everything he had. He gave the Gospel a good reputation.

Everything he had was for the Lord. That outlook is what I remember most about him. He was dedicated to winning souls and planting churches. I have a Bible and a songbook that Mr. Rogers inscribed to my father in staid British handwriting: "To Luis Palau, on our first missionary journey, 1937." That is how my father and Mr. Rogers saw themselves: as missionaries who made a living to keep food on the table so that they could share the Gospel and plant new churches.

My father and Mr. Rogers had a simple church-planting philosophy: make converts, appoint elders, build a chapel, and kiss them all goodbye. And it worked. My dad would tell the new converts with clear leadership and service abilities, "If you hold services for women and children with preaching and the Lord's Supper, I will build you a house so that you can be comfortable and dedicate yourself to be sure that the church grows."

Not only would they build a chapel, they would build the man a house. My view of church leadership was shaped by men like Mr. Rogers and my father, businessmen who loved the Lord and used all their resources to serve him. Not until later in life did I learn that there were dedicated, paid pastors in many churches whose whole profession was to preach and minister. As elders, my father and Mr. Rogers helped to run the church from their own pocketbook.

The two men planted nine churches this way in the communities around Buenos Aires. My sisters and I used to laugh because my dad repeated the same nervous motion when he preached— rising on the balls of his feet in a kind of bounce. In every little town, he would tell the same story of his conversion, with John 3:16 in the featured role: *"Porque de tal manera amó Dios al mundo, que ha dado á su Hijo unigénito, para que todo aquel que en él cree, no se pierda, mas tenga vida eterna."*

And it was always followed by Acts 16:31: *"Cree en el Señor Jesucristo, y serás salvo tú, y tu casa."* "Believe in the Lord Jesus, and you will be saved—you and your household."

My father's lessons to me were not many, but they were key. He showed me the power that comes when a person says, "Everything I have is for the Lord."

When Dad died, the money began to trickle away. Early on, we had no idea how bad it would get. Somehow, I was able to attend another year at Quilmes and then transfer to St. Albans College, a prestigious school in the rich suburbs south of Buenos Aires. We lived north of the city, about an hour and a half (train, subway, train) away. The school was affiliated directly with Cambridge

University's "Overseas" program. St. Albans was also affiliated with the Church of England—quite different from my church background. Our occasional chapel services mostly seemed to center on Philippians 4:8 (an applicable verse for troublemaking boys):

> Whatsoever things are true, whatsoever things are honest, whatsoever things are just, whatsoever things are pure, whatsoever things are lovely, whatsoever things are of good report; if there be any virtue, and if there be any praise, think on these things. (KJV)

The goal of the school was to British-ize you. We played rugby and cricket. Soccer *futbol* as we called it—was not allowed. We played in secret anyway. (Anyone who thinks they can stop an Argentine from kicking a soccer ball is a bit deluded.) The school's faculty members were all Freemasons, with the little caps and all. Graduates were expected to join too, but our church discouraged joining secret societies, and I always thought Freemasonry was an odd way to have a good-ol'-boys club.

The British faculty only allowed us to speak Spanish in the mornings, so my English, which I knew pretty well for a second language, quickly improved. Life at the school was disciplined and a little like the military, with marching and parade drills. Thirty boys shared a room, sleeping on orderly, lined-up beds.

St. Albans had a system of accelerated education that divided the day into two parts. The mornings were taught in Spanish and covered the subjects the Argentine government required. The afternoons were exclusively in English, implementing the Cambridge Overseas program, which was intended to be like a junior college to give students about a two-year head start on their studies by graduation. It was strenuous and intended to feed students into Cambridge University to finish their education. In the program at St. Albans, I decided that I wanted to become a lawyer. I was already a smooth talker and had a gift for helping people see things my way. Even so, I dreamed of preaching and thought about how easy it would be to emulate Dad: he had a profession to make a living and spread the Gospel as a street preacher and a church planter.

I graduated from St. Albans in 1950. Soon after, as the shambles of the family finances made themselves known, I was forced to give up my dreams of law school in England. We moved to Córdoba, I began working at the Bank of London, and the rest of my life began to unfold.

Though my father was only alive until I was ten, his life and death have shaped me as a person and incalculably influenced my ministry. Chief among the lessons that he gave me is simply this: we must give everything we have back to the Lord.

We are the sheep of His pasture, after all. Does not the Shepherd who guides us deserve our best? My father's total and quiet commitment illustrate this beautifully.

Thinking of him forces me to consider what areas of my life I am holding back from the Lord. Perhaps you should consider it too. Some people find it easy to give money to the cause of Jesus but can't *imagine* giving their time—or worse, risking their reputation! Others find volunteering quite easy, but their wallets have not been converted. Are we dedicating ourselves to Christ and His kingdom as whole persons? Is all of us—body, mind, soul, and spirit—being laid at the feet of Jesus?

This powerful question leads us straight into the life of the last remaining giant of my early years, the man whose work led the Palau family to the knowledge of saving faith and the assurance of salvation in Jesus.

CHAPTER 3

Lift High the Light

The Good News of Mr. Charles Rogers

We preach Christ crucified.

1 CORINTHIANS 1:23

The man who had given my mother the Bible was named Mr. Edward Charles Rogers. He was a British businessman who did missionary work on the side—although he would have said that his business was the real side project!

Because Maschwitz was a faded upper-middle-class retreat, the town had an international character. People from France, Belgium, the Netherlands, and Britain made their home there, often commuting into the city for the business or industrial work that brought them to Argentina.

Though many immigrated to Argentina to make money, a surprising number came to evangelize. Most of these evangelists came from the British Isles or its former colonies: England, Scotland, and a few from Wales, as well as Australia and New Zealand. Some focused on preaching, others on teaching and education, but all were missionaries.

Almost all of them were "tentmakers" like the apostle Paul, who supported his missionary work by making tents (see Acts 18:3). These missionaries worked for all kinds of industries: from railroads to the large meat-packing companies that produced Argentina's famous beef. They were not a financial burden on Argentines or people from their home countries, but they quietly gave their spare time to preach, plant churches, mentor local leaders, and lead Bible studies. There was some risk involved for these missionaries. A couple even lost their jobs because of their ministry.

Mr. Rogers came to preach the Gospel and win people to Christ. He and a group of Plymouth Brethren friends—perhaps thirty—came from different parts of the UK: Scotland, Wales, Ireland, England. Even though they all did different types of ministry, they stayed in touch and held an annual Bible conference. We called them missionaries. They didn't. They just called themselves Christians and humbly served. They began near Buenos Aires but eventually spread to other provinces.

The missionaries all had a working knowledge of Spanish, including translation and writing. One had a printing company that printed hymnbooks, tracts, magazines, and even little books of outlines for young preachers.

Mr. Rogers was a high-ranking oil executive. I don't know much about his professional life or history other than that. But on weekends and holidays—and Argentina had many—Mr. Rogers evangelized.

He walked door to door, carrying a heavy walking stick, for Argentina was full of dogs, some stray, some keeping watch over their owners' front yards. He carefully laid out his route so he wouldn't miss anyone. His method wasn't pushy. He simply gave away New Testaments—nice ones with pictures of biblical sites.

"Would you like a copy of the Word of God?" he would ask. And most people would say yes. It was a gift after all!

In my first memory of Mr. Rogers, I only come up to about his knee. He looked so tall and dignified holding his enormous red leather Bible. To me, that book was most impressive—I revered it!

The Plymouth Brethren chapel that Mr. Rogers led was the first real Bible-preaching church in Maschwitz. The chapel was not much to look at. It was made of corrugated metal and measured about twenty by twenty feet—a *tiny* little thing. But it was in that tiny chapel where my mother attended Bible study after her conversion, where my father was converted, and where I have my first memories of church.

But a church is not a building, of course. It is the people. There were not very many of us— not many would have fit in the building!—but we were committed.

The rain comes down hard in Argentina. In the winter when it poured, you could hardly hear the preacher over the rain drumming against the sheet-metal roof and walls. The rain would even drown out our singing. It was like worshiping inside a tin can. But metal was the only thing they had to build with, so we made do.

The whole service was led by the Spirit. One brother would get up and call out, "Let's sing hymn fifty-four." We sang a cappella—which could be pretty bad! But they believed musical accompaniment in church interrupted your meditation. So we just sang. Then someone else would stand up and suggest a passage: "Let's read Isaiah 53." And we would read: "All we like sheep have gone astray . . ." (KJV).

Our worship was simple but profound. Every Sunday we shared the Lord's Supper. Small benches and chairs were pulled around the table, which stood at the center. Children too young to participate sat in the back and watched. It was awesome—a striking worship service every Sunday. It was a powerful experience for me. As a young child, I sat quietly listening to the rustle of clothing, a hushed cough, all the little noises people make when they are trying to keep quiet.

Many Christian traditions celebrate communion with pomp and ceremony. We didn't even have a cross on the wall, but no one took things more seriously than we did in that little sheet-metal building. There were long silences, the whole room hushed in the sacredness of the Lord's Supper. There was no rush to get through the service, no need to get to a song, reading, or prayer. No one watched the clock. There was time, and we meditated on the sacrifice of Jesus. We thought about the cross. Eventually, a man would stand up and recite the familiar words: "The Lord, on the night he was betrayed, took bread, and he broke it." At this, he would tear the loaf into four pieces and pass it among us. We each took a little and ate. Then the one cup—"The blood of Christ, shed for us."

We shared a common loaf and a common cup and experienced the solemnity of passing the cup and the bread between us. We had one huge loaf that represented the body of Christ. We were one body with one loaf.

And we all drank from the same cup. As far as I know, nobody got sick. I was a bit of a smart aleck, though. I knew where the cup started and seated myself in the first spot so that I didn't have to drink after the others.

Some of my earliest memories are sitting in that chapel quietly, solemnly considering the cross, the blood, and the body broken. The church service left a deep impression on me. "My God! My God! Why have you forsaken me?" (Matthew 27:46). "Father forgive them, for they do not know what they are doing." (Luke 23:34). Those solemn thoughts and words became part of my young heart.

Why are Mom and Dad so involved in this? I wondered. *There must be something real here.*

Today there are about thirty-five churches in that area of Maschwitz. When Mr. Rogers first planted a church, it was the only one. Even today, that little church has a small congregation, but through the years, the church has sent forty-four young people into full-time ministry, including me. Tall, quiet Mr. Rogers has impacted the globe.

Our church respected children as full members. They trusted us to understand the deep things of the faith, they encouraged us to grow, they never talked down to us, and they never made us feel less important than the adults. They treated us with respect and expected us to learn doctrine. They didn't treat us like simpletons who only showed up for pizza parties. They treated us like intelligent human beings who *wanted* to know God, *needed* to know God, and *could* know God.

One of the great things about my upbringing was that, despite how "separatist" our church community was, Mr. Rogers never put others down. Despite all the problems that we suffered in our relationships with nominal Catholics, he never attacked other churches. We clarified and detailed our distinct doctrine, but we were always charitable. Sometimes we would hear other preachers blast the Catholics for their doctrines not found in the Bible—worship of the Virgin Mary, the intercession of the saints, and the rest—which do distract from the Good News of Jesus.

But not Mr. Rogers. "Tell the truth," he'd say. "Tell of the glorious light of God, and the darkness of Satan flees. Just turn on the light in a dark room and see what happens. The light always outshines the darkness. The darkness cannot overcome it. Preach the light. Always the light. It can take care of itself." Jesus Christ can stand on His own, and Mr. Rogers did not need to attack others to defend Jesus.

Mr. Rogers didn't pull punches in his preaching, though. He hammered home the reality of the corruption of the human heart. Mr. Rogers tied all the ills that burdened society back to the reality of sin. From the sinful heart came everything bad, everything from a broken marriage to global poverty. Murder, violence, war, loneliness, despair—all came from the same dark place inside. Everything wrong was a result of sin. Yet, Mr. Rogers would preach, there was no condemnation—only free forgiveness and a love that triumphs over the darkness inside and outside us.

Through Mr. Rogers's preaching, I came to realize my heart was also deceitful and desperately wicked. Such powerful sentiments helped clear the ground in my heart and mind so that the truth of God could be built on a firm foundation.

Out of those little meetings, nine churches were planted in the surrounding small towns. As my father's truck drove through the street, we kids would throw flyers from the truck bed, inviting people to a meeting to hear the Gospel. At the meeting, Mr. Rogers would preach, my dad would tell his story, and my mother would sing. Meanwhile, we kids would weave through the crowd passing out literature. "Have one of these!" I'd say. "Go read it." Some accepted our gift, and some teased or outright insulted us. We got used to the range of responses that people have in a situation like that.

Every summer, Mr. Rogers and my father chose a new town to

preach in. For the duration of the summer, they would preach on the streets and gather new converts. Then as the year closed, they would appoint elders for a new church, and my father would build them a simple chapel, complete with a baptistery and an outhouse. The nine churches they planted still exist today as a testament to their ministry. I have visited some of them with my sons, and it was powerful to see that legacy continue.

I was a restless little fellow. My mom made me sit in the front row at church—so that I'd listen. From a kid's perspective, Mr. Rogers's face was half covered by the Bible as he preached, just the hint of his neatly trimmed British moustache—quite dapper—peeking out from behind the pages. Even in summer, he dressed like a proper Brit in a full vest, jacket, and tie. The sweat poured from his brow as he preached. And we were all thinking, *The apostles didn't wear a vest and jacket. Why do you need to?*

When I think about Mr. Rogers, what first comes to mind is his solemnity before the cross and his utter dependence upon the Word. The Lord put His story in writing so that we wouldn't forget it. We hold the same Word of the Lord that the apostles passed to their followers. We must return to it constantly.

There is a picture of the tent that Mr. Rogers led meetings in. They would put the tent up so people could see it from the highway. Beside it, on a sign longer than the tent, were huge painted letters: WE PREACH CHRIST CRUCIFIED. Since I was a boy, the central place of the cross in the Gospel has defined my understanding of what it means to be a Christian.

The first sermon I remember preaching was from Psalm 1. I was preaching at a Sunday afternoon youth meeting. I was eighteen years old. In theory, the service was for youth, but in practice, everybody showed up. That service was probably the most fun of all our weekly services. By most standards, it was still pretty uptight. But by our church's standards, it was lighthearted and amusing.

I prepared furiously for the sermon, poring over the Bible, writing copious notes, even copying Charles Spurgeon's commentary on Psalm 1. I thought I had enough material for forty-five minutes. But the time flew by in a blur, and I finished my last point in ten minutes.

I was humiliated! I blew through everything that I wanted to say (most of which had been lifted shamelessly from Spurgeon), and I stood behind the pulpit in front of a silent church. I don't remember how I ended it, but my clumsy conclusion took two minutes, bringing the total length of my first sermon to precisely twelve minutes. I had wanted to do so well. But it was still a good experience. Let's just say we can all be glad I got better as a preacher.

Unfortunately, we lost touch with Mr. Rogers when we moved from Maschwitz to Córdoba. After my father died, Mr. Rogers helped immensely. He and another friend did all they could to patch together the shambles of our finances and protect us from the worst cases of cheating that they discovered. Mr. Rogers ended up personally renting our Maschwitz home for a very generous amount to help provide a steady stream of income for my mother.

Of all the lessons I learned from Mr. Rogers, one stands out with striking clarity: *preach the light.*

I had an autograph book as a lad. It was the custom. If you handed the book to a big shot, they'd sign it. I took it to Mrs. Rogers before we moved to Córdoba. Mrs. Rogers worked very closely with her husband. She was always dressed properly like a classic middle-aged Englishwoman. Both she and Mr. Rogers loved and valued children. What she put on the page of my autograph book illustrates their contribution to my life better than any words I can describe.

She drew a cottage in the corner of one page. The tiny house sat lonely in the dark. But out from its window poured tremendous beams of light, lighting up the darkness. Under the picture, she wrote, "Let your light shine," quoting the words of our Lord Jesus in Matthew 5:16.

That picture was so vivid that even then I took it as a message from the Lord. I was supposed to take the light to the darkness. Everything I saw reminded me of evangelism. When you were around evangelists, they lived for one thing: to share the Gospel.

When I try to think of more personal stories, more specific impressions of the man, I find I cannot. Mr. Rogers is one-dimensional in my boyhood memories—a preacher and an evangelist with a carefully groomed moustache, limitless solemn sincerity, and a big red Bible. Mr. Rogers is a reminder that sometimes God may use us in a one-dimensional way in a person's life. When I look back, I realize that I didn't know Mr. Rogers as much as I imagined I knew him. I was a child after all, and children feel like they know everyone around them well. I was too young to understand much about his life. Today, I have a hundred questions I would like to ask him. Then, I simply took it for granted that a high-ranking executive of a major foreign oil company would use his weekends to help lead our tiny church.

I wonder how many people like Mr. Rogers have impacted your life? Who was the pivotal hinge that helped swing your life toward God? Who reminds you of the Lord every time that you think of them?

My conversion was very simple—a boy receiving the Lord with little in the way of nastiness to be saved from. There's not much to it. You certainly couldn't make a movie out of it. No murderous sprees, no drug-fueled rampages to be saved from—none of the *colorful* stuff.

But as I tell the many people I know who have similarly "unremarkable" conversions, the very commonplace nature of it is part of what makes it so miraculous. Our human sense of drama expects sweeping acts of redemption and a wild story. What about the boy at camp who is simply grieving the loss of his father? For God to plant something real and fierce and undeniable in that awkward little fellow—that is a miracle to rival any jailhouse testimony in history.

Intellectually, I believed in God, as many children do. The fact that I'd never known a life apart from attending and worshiping in our little church certainly helped prepare me. Nevertheless, I was becoming my own person capable of independent thought, of independent choice, of real acceptance or rejection of the truth. I had made no formal commitment of faith. The Anglican church connected to my boarding school had confirmation classes, but it was quite high church, and I don't remember much about the classes leading up to the confirmation.

I remember the confirmation ceremony as a solemn and sacred-feeling moment. Sure, we goofed and joked and made unflattering (and imaginative!) remarks about the bishop. But when it came time for him to do his job, we took it seriously. The bishop, dressed in impressive robes, laid his hand on my head. He said a few words, prayed over me, and moved on to the next kid. Every student did it because *every student did it*. To me it was an important moment—I took it seriously, like with anything having to do with the Lord—but the bishop's words, like his hand, just sat on top of my head. The true confirmation needed to happen in my heart.

My true conversion came in February 1947 during a

two-week-long camp. During the first week of camp, they had a Bible teacher in the morning, and another talk in the evening, and in between we played lots of old-fashioned British games like cricket and rounders. One teacher was responsible to talk us boys through the topic of sex—back then they avoided directly talking about it, and he made the most confusing mess of the conversation, talking about bees and birds and trees that grow straight, until we had not the first idea of what he was saying, other than that what he was trying to tell us about sounded *much* more interesting than he was letting on. It was intended to teach us purity, and if purity had come through sheer confusion, it would have worked. As it was, his sense of godliness was real, and it inspired me, but I could not have told you a word he said or what it meant, other than in the vaguest terms.

There were seven boys and a counselor to each large army tent. The second week of camp, after we'd all gone to bed, the counselor of each tent would take each boy out for a one-on-one conversation. My counselor, Frank Chandler, left me till the last night. When we left the tent, the wind was whipping up a bit, and rain seemed imminent.

We walked to a fallen log not that far from the tent, but far enough away to have a private conversation. "Luis," Frank said as we sat down, "if you were to die tonight, would you go to heaven or hell?"

I knew the Bible too well to fudge on that question. "I'd go to hell," I said.

"Why?" he asked.

I thought of all the ways that I fell short. "Well, I have a foul attitude," I began, "a dirty mouth, a bad temper, I swear a lot when things don't go my way, and I'm not that nice to my sisters."

"Okay, then," he said. "But is hell where you want to go?"

"No!" I said. "I want to go to heaven."

"Do you know what you need to do?"

"Yes," I replied. "Believe in the Lord Jesus Christ."

"Yes," he said. "Let me read to you." He turned to Romans 10:9 and 10, reading them in the thin yellow beam from his flashlight.

I'd heard those verses a million times. But they took on new meaning that night. "What does this say to *you?*" he asked.

"That I have to confess with my mouth."

"Do you believe in your heart that God raised Jesus from the dead?" he asked.

"Yes, I do," I replied.

"Okay," he said, "listen." He read the verse again then but personalized the passage by putting my name into it. "If you, Luis, confess with your mouth, Luis, that Jesus is Lord, and believe in your heart, Luis, that God raised Him from the dead, then you, Luis, shall be saved."

For some reason, that was all it really took. The Gospel in that moment was not an abstract truth; it was completely personal, utterly meaningful to me. Jesus was Lord! Not only of the world but of *Luis.* I believed it—yes, I did.

"Will you confess Him?" he asked.

"Yes," I said.

It was raining—the first big drops threatening a real summer storm. Frank continued reading, trying to shelter the thin pages of his Bible from the weather, and then he prayed with me.

I laugh about it now—that because of the storm I felt a bit rushed during my moment of decision. But it was real. I knew immediately that something was different. Something in me changed and came to life. I remember running back through the rain into the tent calling out to the boys on their cots, "I've got eternal life! I've got eternal life!"

There wasn't much drama to it on the surface. Just a camp counselor walking a kid through the Bible, sitting on a log one rainy night in Argentina.

You don't have to have a jaw-dropping story of how you received Jesus. It just must be *yours*. Some have the light falling from heaven, the Damascus road experience that takes them from the "chief of sinners" into the arms of Jesus. Some of us are kids just starting to learn what sin means, and the light from heaven looks like a shaky flashlight beam on the page of a Bible as chilly rain falls around. All that is important in our conversion is the reality of it. All that's important is saying, personally and from the heart, that Jesus is *your* Lord, knowing that God raised Him from the dead not only for the world but *for you*.

Though I'd gone to church since I was still kicking in the womb, that was the moment I chose Christ for myself. And from that moment, I have never doubted.

Luis has eternal life.

Years later, I traveled to an evangelistic festival in the island province of Tierra del Fuego in southern Argentina, some fifteen hundred miles south of where I grew up and just a stone's throw from Antarctica. I landed at the airport in the province's capital, Ushuaia. While I was getting my bags, a young man walked up and asked, "Hey, Palau—is that you?"

"Yes," I replied.

"Did you know that Mr. Rogers, who led your family to Christ, is buried here?"

I was surprised by the odd greeting, and a little stunned. "I had no idea," I said. "Nobody ever told us what happened to him after his wife died." We had all just assumed that Mr. Rogers had returned to his home country.

Here is the real story, as I found out from my childhood friend Ronny, who had remained in Mr. Rogers church. At some point after we'd moved away, Mr. Rogers's wife died. After his wife's death, Mr. Rogers continued to minister in our little church in Maschwitz. After a little while, however, he began to talk about Southern Argentina. "They have no Bible church there," he told the other elders. "Not one. Someone has to go—to take Bibles and begin a church." Everyone agreed. But time passed and nobody went. Finally, Mr. Rogers gathered the elders for a meeting, where he announced that he was going to Ushuaia in Tierra del Fuego. He had gotten older and wasn't in the best of health. The elders all protested: "You mustn't go! One of us will."

"You've been saying that for years," he replied. "Nobody's going. I can tell that none of you are determined. I am, and I'm going. If I die there, I die there. But I am going to go."

So he went. He had very little money at that point. As he traveled, he prayed for God to provide what he needed. On arriving, he met a group of nuns. Mr. Rogers went to them and said, "I need a place to stay. If you give me a room and a bed and can feed me, I'll give you what little money I have, and I'll teach you English." And they agreed! So he lived in a convent, slept on a cot, and ate his meals among the sisters. And he spent his days going door to door, giving the book of Proverbs and the Gospel of John to anyone who would take them.

From his simple evangelism, the same quiet method that led my own family to Jesus, a church was founded. To my knowledge, the church was the first evangelical congregation in that area. Not long after the church began, Mr. Rogers passed into the next life.

I visited his grave. I knelt beside it, so distant from the United Kingdom where this man had been raised. I remembered his moustache, his red Bible, his accented voice ringing with clear kindness in the little sheet-metal chapel. *Just shine the light*, I thought. *Just shine the light.* I thanked God for him from the bottom of my heart and pondered the lengths he had gone to give his life away for the

Good News. It was very moving. He had lived for Christ. His life was burned out in the service of God. His practically unknown grave here at the world's end was a paltry testament. His true memorial was elsewhere—in me, in the many lives he touched, and in the millions of lives touched by those he touched. Mr. Rogers lived to train others to share the Gospel. His gifting was great—he could have had a high-profile ministry had he chosen. But instead he dedicated himself to others, lifting them up, training them, and growing by multiplying disciples of Jesus Christ instead of adding to his own platform. Mr. and Mrs. Rogers were relentless. They poured their energy into their mission. They chose to come to Argentina. They paid for their own ministry. They even spent their own money on us. What dedication! What love! Mr. Rogers's passion for the lost still inspires me. He left England for Buenos Aires, Buenos Aires for Tierra del Fuego, and he poured his life out lavishly. Why? Because people needed the Good News. It didn't matter that his finances dwindled, that his situation was hard, that he died seemingly unknown. He gave his life with single-minded devotion. That stable single-mindedness is his greatest lesson to me. If a double-minded man is unstable, a single-minded man is stable in all his ways. Faithful to the end.

CHAPTER 4

The Freedom
of a Father

Ray Stedman and the Joyful

Strength of the Gospel

You will know the truth, and the truth will set
you free.

JOHN 8:32

In Córdoba, I found a job at a branch of the Bank of London. It was an old-fashioned building, like something you'd see in a film, all metal and hardwoods, with the tellers sitting in little cage-like booths, the mechanical sounds of typewriter keys and bells filling the air.

Had I sat up front very often, I might have started to feel like a caged animal. But I only got called up front to cash checks and take deposits when we were short staffed. Because I was bilingual,

I worked mostly behind the scenes on international banking deals. For example, if the city wanted to buy six street-sweeping machines from Detroit, then I was their man. I figured out the documentation, calculated the exchange rate, and smiled while I was at it. I had a good mind for business, just like Dad.

It wasn't a bad job, and I learned a lot about how nations and people relate. I paid attention to memos circulated by other branches of our bank from far-off places like New York. That job made me more confident and more internationally minded. But by the time I had left, I hated the smell of money with a passion.

My weeks were punctuated by periodic promises from my boss that I was being trained to be a manager and, of course, *payday*. Payday was the one time in the month I could splurge a bit for my mom and sisters. My salary was small, but I'd always buy a box of chocolates to take home.

We'd open the box and start our customary game—I'd portion out the sweets based on which of the sisters could say *chocolat* with the most hilariously over-the-top pronunciation. They'd draw out the word—"*Choc-o-laaaat*"—like characters from a soap opera, and we'd laugh and laugh.

Sure, we laughed a lot on payday, but deep inside I felt a brewing bitterness about our finances. I was helping others make deals and counting cash at the end of the day. It sure seemed to me that a well-padded bank account offered real freedom.

"Luis," my Scottish grandfather would say, "you love money too much. Watch out. It's going to destroy you if you're not careful." He wasn't a believer, but he must have seen some dangerous glint of gold in my eye.

Our church in Córdoba held a Tuesday evening Bible study. After my day at the bank, I'd hop on my little black German motorbike and ride the whining machine through the back streets to the church. Sometimes I'd get there a little early and find three or four little old widowed ladies and one man who could hardly walk, all of whom had come early to pray. I loved to get there before the service to talk to them. Something about our conversations was inexpressibly encouraging to me. They seemed to talk to me not just as a teenage nuisance screeching in on a loud motorbike but as a real person who was quickly becoming a man with something to give to the church.

My life at the bank and my life at our little church couldn't have been more different. Looking back, I can see that there was an invisible struggle between a version of Luis who longed to be a brilliant and successful businessman and a version of Luis who felt an undeniable call to tell the world about Jesus.

When I was eighteen, the choice—which was more about my heart than my occupation—came to the surface in a colorful way. As a boy, I'd read about a missionary who'd contracted leprosy on the mission field. I was haunted by the story. One day, I felt the Lord asking a simple question: *Luis, are you willing to give your life for the sake of others? Are you willing to get leprosy for Me?*

I could tell He meant it. I paced around and thought, *Wow, Lord. Really?* Leprosy is horrible today. It was worse back then when there was no effective treatment. Years later, I would visit a leper colony in Colombia, and the weight of the question hit me again. By the time I visited the leper colony, some remedies for the disease had been discovered, thank God. Even so, the ravages of the disease were evident—fingers missing, noses gone.

The question became a crisis for me—I knew that I couldn't answer it dishonestly. What mattered was that I considered the commitment. Counted the cost.

Finally, peace replaced my tension, and I knew the honest answer. *Lord, I'll do whatever You ask. Even if it means risking leprosy for the sake of the Good News, I'll do it.*

It was a moment of surrender. A moment of becoming a "living sacrifice." I'd like to say that it was a revelation, a glorious high point of faith. Instead, it felt like throwing up my hands exhausted after wrestling with a God who was much better at a tussle than I was. I suppose it was only fair. I was a teen. He was the Lord of the Universe.

Around that time, I was asked to speak to the elders of our church.

"Luis," they said gravely, "we need you to explain something to us."

My mind raced, trying to think of *anything* that would merit a conversation like this.

"Okay," I said. "What is it?"

They looked at each other. "Somebody saw you standing in front of a *cinema*," one finally said. "Looking at the posters." He paused, gauging my reaction. "Did you go in and watch a film?"

I was furious. *What on earth?* I thought. *These guys think they can tell me where I can stop on the sidewalk?* The church's rules against watching movies in those days certainly felt constricting sometimes, but this was absurd.

"I didn't see a movie," I told them passionately.

"Then why were you standing there, Luis?"

None of your fat business, was what I wanted to say. Praise God, I held back my temper and said, "If you want to know so badly, I'll tell you."

I had stopped in front of that movie theater because I had been paying close attention to Billy Graham, who'd just led his 1957 crusade in New York, even preaching in Times Square. A friend working with the crusade bundled the weekly bulletins from the campaign and mailed them to me. I had been poring over them, fascinated by the great evangelist's deft usage of everything from philosophy to pop culture when preaching to the great metropolis. Mr. Graham had even managed to frame his sermon around three current movie titles.

I had stopped to look at the movie titles, turning them over in my mind for angles to preach from. How ironic that my elders would look down their noses at me as I was considering how to preach effectively to an audience outside the walls of our church! I wouldn't have even *thought* of going to a movie in those days because the church considered it to be "worldly." Not only that, but my mother agreed with them, and I couldn't disappoint her.

They accepted my explanation with a bit of suspicion. And I left with a bit of my own

This is probably why, not long after, I didn't bother to ask the elders' permission to go hear a pair of Americans in town to do some preaching. An acquaintance had slipped me an invitation at the bank. Our church frowned upon preachers from other churches, but I felt like I needed a bit of fresh overseas air. The photo in the paper showed Dick Hillis, the former number-three executive of China Inland Mission and a prisoner in Communist China for two years, and Ray Stedman, a pastor from Peninsula Bible Church in California. What caught my attention was the word *California*. That name only meant one thing to me in those days—*Hollywood*—and I immediately wanted to go see this man from that magical land. A *Bible church in Hollywood?* I thought, and in that moment the decision was made. And I didn't tell anyone I was going.

The evening gripped me. Dick Hillis's story of survival and protection was amazing. He'd even been saved by angels when Chairman Mao was at his most threatening. He was about as strait-laced as a Biola University grad can be—not the kind to go around telling stories of miraculous deliverance willy-nilly!

Then Ray came on. Apparently he was a well-known preacher

and writer. I can't remember exactly what he talked about. I only remember *how* he talked. He was so joyful, so winsome. His message was stridently biblical, but so different than the elders who would have disapproved of me being there. His words were natural and beautiful. I liked him immediately. I watched and listened closely, trying to figure out what I admired so that I could imitate it. Whatever he had, I wanted it. He was a man's man, free, easy to laugh. He loved God, but it was obvious he had *fun*. He preached the same Gospel as the church that had raised me, but watching him, you could just see that it was *Good* News.

I wanted to meet this guy.

After the meeting, I went to the lobby, still looking over my shoulders for fear I'd see the elders trailing me in trench coats. While I was standing there, Ray came up and just started talking. I think he was relieved to find someone who spoke English, and though my accent was awful, we got to know each other just fine.

If questions were bullets, Ray Stedman carried around a machine gun: "Who are you? Where do you work? Where do you go to church? Are you married? Have a girlfriend?"

His next question was more of an invitation. "Tomorrow morning, I'm having a Bible study at a missionary's home," he said. "Do you want to come?"

I did. The next morning, I rode my motorbike through Córdoba to the home of a missionary named Keith Bentson. I had never been in the home of a missionary before and was curious to see what it looked like. I don't know what I expected, but I hadn't expected its completely unremarkable interior. *Huh. Just a normal home*, I thought.

But the teacher was anything but normal, for me at least. Ray taught on the "Salt of the Earth, Light of the World." The high point for me came when he broke out into a little ditty:

To dwell above
With saints we love,
Why that would all be glory.
To dwell below,
With saints we know,
Now that's another story.

To use humor during a sermon would have been unthinkable! But to say something like *that?* It was clever and humorous, sure. But it was also *true.* My experience with the elders fit right into "another story." Ray's confidence and freedom seemed hewn from a deep inner peace. He didn't seem afraid of sin. He wasn't obsessed with following anyone's artificial rules. He simply loved God and was comfortable in his own skin.

With that, one of the great teachers of my life began to teach me one of the great lessons of my life. I saw that the Good News was not all solemnity and keeping the rules. It was more than good doctrine and handing out tracts and testimonies. It could be laughed and lived. The Gospel was not a burden. It was freedom, true freedom, Galatians chapter 5 freedom.

As people began to leave after the meeting, Ray came up to me and said, "Luis, will you take me out on your motorbike? I want to buy presents for my girls."

"Why would you buy something in Argentina?" I asked. "All our stuff is made in Hong Kong."

"Aw, I want to take them a few mementoes," he said. Before I knew it, my little motorbike was coughing through the streets of Córdoba, struggling under our combined weight—Ray was not a small man.

Along the way, his questions just kept coming. "What do you want to do?" he called over the noise of traffic. "What are your goals? What are you planning?"

"I want to serve the Lord," I said.

"Ever thought about going to the States for school?"

"I think about it," I said. "The missionaries loan me *Moody* magazine and stuff like that. But I couldn't leave my mom and sisters."

But he wouldn't shut up. He went on and on about how America was the place to go for training.

I kept trying to convince him to buy something better for his family than the junk they sold at the little tourist stops, but my mystification at his poor souvenir choices didn't faze him. As I dropped him off after our journey, he looked at me. "I'm going back to the USA in the morning," he said. "Come by and say goodbye tomorrow. And pray about coming to the States."

I smiled, mostly just to pacify him. "Okay, I will." After all, what could a little prayer hurt?

My mother had remarried, though it was a complicated relationship. She and my new stepfather had a son, Jorge. And I had my little brother Jorge in tow at the airport the next morning.

Ray looked glad to see us. We chatted a bit as he waited to board. Finally it was time to go. "Luis," he said, "I'm going to pray for you. I'll write you too. Come to the States."

"Maybe someday, God willing," I said, glancing at my brother. "But I have to take care of my family."

"God *is* going to will it," he said. "The money will come for you and your mother. Don't worry. It is the Lord's will that you come."

The strength of his assertion stuck with me. He seemed confident not only that God *could* do it but that He *wanted* to. For the first time, it struck me that traveling to the United States might be a possibility. But still, I wondered, *How could he say all that?*

Ray promised to write, and it didn't take him long. Just hours, in fact. I was surprised just shortly afterward by a Pan-American mailgram, sent by Ray from the tarmac of the airport in Caracas, Venezuela, where his plane had stopped before flying the long leg to Miami:

GET READY AND GET A PASSPORT.
THE LORD IS GOING TO BRING YOU TO THE
STATES.

I only vaguely knew what a passport was, but I began to feel that maybe there was something to his certainty.

Laughing a little, I showed the mailgram to my mother. "Hey, Mom, look at this," I said, handing her the mailgram. "This fellow thinks I'm heading to the USA." I explained everything to her briefly. She didn't seem particularly surprised. "But I can't go," I finished. "I need to support you and the girls and Jorge."

"If it's the Lord's will, then everything will work out," she said with confidence.

Her trust and openness were what I needed. If she had discouraged or dismissed the idea, I don't think I would have ever gone.

But I got my passport.

I was used to thinking of pastors as either bivocational or the poorest people on earth. It didn't seem like a remote possibility that a pastor could pay my way to the States, let alone help put me through school.

What I didn't know then was that Ray sat on the board of a foundation started by the man who'd been involved with the invention of a little appliance called the microwave oven. Ray had connections, and those connections had money. Bring-Luis-to-the-States money. People cooking microwave dinners around the world had no idea that they were helping connect the dots between a kid in Córdoba, Argentina, and the USA.

Not long after I got my passport, a check came. From that point on, things accelerated so quickly that I felt I had to slap my face in the mirror to ensure I was awake. Before I knew it, plans had been made and a one-way ticket had been bought. Destination: San Francisco, where I'd stay for the summer before going north to Oregon and Multnomah School of the Bible.

The goodbyes in Argentina were hard. Family, dear friends, mentors, a girlfriend. Saying goodbye to my mother was hardest. I remembered the words from the time of my father's death that I was the man of the family. How could I leave? But I saw in my mother's eyes that she really wanted me to go. This was following the dream, the call—hers as well as mine. I knew that the step of faith we were taking belonged to all of us. My step of faith was to go without them. Their step of faith was to stay without me. God would provide for all of us.

So, with many promises to stay in touch, to be safe, to learn and grow, I boarded my first airplane.

In those days, flying was an event. They gave you stylishly designed maps with your route laid out. I'd be flying Pan American up South America to the States and then transfer to Delta for a flight across the USA. For a poor kid from Córdoba, it felt like I was living in one of those Hollywood movies that my church's elders disapproved of. It felt glamorous, exciting. I loved it.

The flight was a harrowing experience. Planes flew low in those days, and it was a fearful flight over the mountains. We flew from Buenos Aires to La Paz, La Paz to Lima, Lima to Panama, and Panama to Miami. I couldn't tell where I was as I looked out the window. But I got the impression that the world was very large, which overwhelmed and excited me beyond words.

The last leg to Florida was an overnight flight. When we reached the Caribbean, the sun was beginning to rise. It was June. The weather was beautiful. As I looked down from the window of the plane, I saw countless white shapes dotting the water. *Sailboats!* I thought with a little thrill. Only when I realized our altitude and how it affected my perspective did I realize that those dots were clouds, skimming like ships above the waves.

By the time I landed on American soil in Miami, I was exhausted. The Florida summer humidity tested even my Argentine constitution. But I stumbled, sweaty, through customs, and on June 20, 1960, my Argentine passport was stamped for entry into the United States.

I was overwhelmed with the awesome feeling of coming to the USA, but I still can't remember the details of that first landing. Someone met me at the airport and took me home for a brief rest. Then I went back to the airport—to Atlanta and then San Francisco, where Ray's wife, Elaine, picked me up, greeting me warmly and enthusiastically and clearly in a hurry.

The church service had already started at Peninsula Bible Church, she explained, and she rushed to make it back. She drove me south along the water on the Bayshore Freeway, a causeway crossing part of the San Francisco Bay. We flew over the new road—doing seventy miles per hour most of the way.

We made it before the service ended, but barely. I was whisked up to the stage to be introduced, my travel-weary mind barely comprehending the words, *Welcome to Luis Palau from Argentina!* I said a few words, thanked them for their welcome, and quietly marveled at where I found myself.

That summer, I stayed in the Stedman's home. Seeing Ray in the context of his church, family, and community gave me opportunities to see that he was the real deal. Ray's laughter and love for Jesus were contagious. His life was given to Christ and the church, and he also seemed to be enjoying himself. He played golf—terribly, but he played anyway! He fished. He was no good at fishing either.

But he *did* it. And people respected him and loved him for who he really was because he shared his real self. He was loving and genuine and a man's man.

I wanted to be like that.

I worked to learn the American culture. In those days, American Christians didn't drink alcohol. They just didn't. That was so different from the moderate drinking that Christians enjoyed in Argentina. While I was still in Córdoba, one missionary had counseled me: "Luis, don't *ever* ask for a drink of wine up there. It's normal here, but American believers don't touch it."

About the second night in his home, Ray said, "Hey, Luis—let's do an Argentine-style barbecue for you. It's not going to be exactly how you're used to it, but it'll be fun." Then, almost as an afterthought, he added, "Oh, by the way—when you barbecue, do you drink wine?"

My heartrate increased. *Oh man, here we go,* I thought, bracing myself for another talking-to from an elder. "Well," I said, trying to steer the conversation away from the bottle of wine, "you know, Argentina is Europeanized. People will have half a glass of wine with a meal, sure. Even when you're twelve, your grandma pours you a bit—with soda water to cut it."

"Look, kid," he said in his no-nonsense way. "I didn't ask you whether Argentine grandmas drank wine, I asked if *you* drink."

Gosh, I thought. *One night in town and he's grilling me.* "I'll tell you what," I said, squirming a bit. "My mom is not well, so the doctor recommended she drink port wine with a raw egg for her health."

"Not asking if your mother drinks either. Do *you* drink wine with your meat?" He was staring me down at this point. There was no way around. I had to go through.

"Yes, I do."

"Ha! Then let's get a bottle!" he shouted gleefully. We jumped in the car and drove to pick up a bottle of nice red wine, laughing all the way. He'd been testing me for sure. He knew I was sweating at the interrogation, but he was just playing with me. Then I knew, *really* knew, that I liked Ray Stedman. He loved his Jesus and hated legalism.

He was going to be fun.

I lived with Ray the following summer too, as part of something he called "The Scribe's School." I went through it with two others—one of them a young man named Chuck Swindoll. Ray mentored us closely, even allowing us to observe and pray as he did pastoral counseling. With the counselee's permission, I simply sat in the background and listened, not saying a word.

At one point, a well-off couple having marital troubles came in. The husband, an old-school businessman who was not a believer, had brought a check for five thousand dollars written out to the church. He had probably thrown money at problems his entire life and didn't have any other way of dealing with things. At any rate, he made the mistake of sliding the check across the desk to Ray as I sat watched from the back of the room.

Ray read the check. Then he looked the man dead in the eye, tore the check into quarters, and slid it back. "Keep your d—check," he said. "You think you're going to buy God's grace with money?" And with that ferocious kind of gentleness that only an expert pastor has, he laid into the man. I couldn't believe it.

After his counseling, we'd go to lunch at his regular spot, a place called Ricky's on El Camino Real. He'd have a spring in his step all the way. "Ray," I asked once, "how can you counsel people with such deep problems—dark stuff!—all morning and then just seem to shake it off?"

"Hey, if I had to carry their burdens, I'd collapse," he said. "I'm just the Lord's spokesman. I'm there to listen, to help any way that I can, to point them to the Bible. I can help support them and guide them to what will help. But I'm not God. Only He can truly carry their load."

I learned a big lesson in that moment. None of us, however well-meaning, can take the place of savior in a person's life. Only Jesus can do that. We can be present and help. We can listen, speak, support. But if we try to take the place of Jesus in another person's life, we will be crushed by a weight that only He can carry.

This was part of how, years later, I was emotionally able to do *Night Talk with Luis Palau*, our late-night TV program. People would call in with their problems on live television, sometimes bringing major, heavy issues, to be counseled in the midnight hours. I saw myself as washing their feet, like Jesus would. And then, as hard as it sometimes was, I had to move on. I had to trust the Holy Spirit to do the rest.

By displaying his walk with God, Ray shaped and moved me. *Authentic Christianity* was his key book, and it was well titled. Ray's authenticity gave him a magnetic ability to draw others closer to Jesus as Ray himself drew closer to the Savior.

Ray was one of the great pastors of America, but his humility was remarkable. He was always fighting this misty enemy he called the "ego," and that battle was one of the great lessons he gave to me. At the church of my youth, the "world" had been the enemy. Ray made the stakes even higher. The real danger, pride, was *inside* us.

Ray made it clear that one could be the most legalistically righteous person on the earth, and if it puffed you up, you were *nothing* in the kingdom. Of course, personal holiness was vital, but it started with humility of heart, and no amount of false righteousness could counterfeit that. All glory must go to God. "Crucify your ego or it will destroy you," he'd say.

This set up a fascinating juxtaposition in Ray. He distrusted himself and his own pride profoundly. Yet he was completely comfortable being himself.

He would sometimes tell edgy stories or jokes in his sermons—they never really crossed the line to be improper but went *right* up to it—salty language and all. But the Bay area was wild in those days, and he was speaking in a way that his audience understood. He wasn't some disconnected preacher. He knew that free love and LSD were fast taking over the lifestyle of San Francisco, and if he couldn't speak freely in preaching about Jesus, he would miss speaking to the very people who needed to hear about Him the most.

Think about how that would have first struck me, the kid for whom the pulpit had always been a place of absolute seriousness. Sacred stuff. You don't cross *any* lines. Even uttering the word *sex* was taboo. Imagine me, sitting there in the early days, listening to Ray preach on the words of Jesus, "Judge not that ye be not judged," but preached from a thoroughly modern vocabulary.

I'd learned quite a bit of colorful verbiage from my years at boarding school, but hearing Ray's raw language connect with hurting people made me think about preaching in a new way. It made me uncomfortable, sure. But it also was *real* in a way that fascinated me. Most preachers even today wouldn't say the kind of things he said in the pulpit. But there it was acceptable. Biblical to the core, with the rough edges intact.

And it connected. At one point, Ray was preaching through 1 Corinthians. He reached the "such were some of you" passage listing a grievous collection of sins and acknowledging that those sins were in the past lives of many Christians. "How many here are guilty of something on this list?" Ray asked. Many in the room stood up, including a venerable older woman, the widow of a rich Texan, that most people called "the Purple Lady" because of the color choice of her wardrobe.

A hippie had wandered in off the streets, obviously high on something and talking to himself. Early in the sermon, he'd been muttering about all Christians being hypocrites. By the time the Purple Lady began to shout out her testimony, list her sins, and say how Christ had forgiven her, the young man, moved, said, "Man, these are my kind of people!" This was real faith, not empty religiosity. The church was for a time and place where anything went, and the church's wisdom in adapting to that situation was the result of the Holy Spirit's leading their congregation into honesty and simple encouragement.

Still, this congregation may have been that hippie's kind of people, but it was a culture shock for me. My straitlaced background was suspicious of pulpit humor, and this freewheeling California church was decidedly different. Of all the places in the world I could have gone, moving from Buenos Aires to Berkeley seemed calculated to give young Luis the most cultural whiplash. Within just a few years Timothy Leary would be preaching about the benefits of drugs to the youth of California, saying, "Tune in, turn on, drop out." And the kids did it.

It was a shock, but it was also what I needed. The Gospel had been in our dour preaching in Argentina, but I immediately saw that it was here too. The new style wasn't wrong, even if it made me uncomfortable at first. It was just different. And it reached everyone, from professors at Stanford University to the addicts on the streets.

I never became quite as edgy as Ray in the pulpit—though I can tell a gritty story or two. But I felt a new kind of permission to listen to the Holy Spirit and let him lead me to tailor the way that I presented the unchanging Gospel to my audience. That freedom would be needed in the decades to come. One cannot preach widely without adapting how you communicate Jesus with your audience in mind. I am grateful for Ray's fatherly example. His freedom helped me find mine.

He was a father to me and saw our relationship that way as well. At one point, he came to me and offered to adopt me legally. What an honor. I was floored. I turned him down, thinking of my mother and the impossibility of replacing my father. It just didn't feel right. But I knew that in many ways, Ray had adopted me already.

In 1 Corinthians 4:15–16, Paul writes, "Even if you had ten thousand guardians in Christ, you do not have many fathers, for in Christ Jesus I became your father through the gospel. Therefore I urge you to imitate me."

Ray comes to mind when I read this passage. I was a young man who grew up without a father. The experience grew me up fast, but it was still so hard. Very difficult. I had longed for a figure who could do more than just teach me what it meant to be a man—who could *show* me. It had felt as if I had to forge my own way forward, and I was always left with nagging questions. *Is this how I ought to be doing it? Am I becoming a good man?* Though I had a few father figures in and around our family, none of them so completely represented what it meant to be a godly man as Ray did. I wanted to imitate him.

Imitation did not mean copying. It meant imitating his freedom. It meant learning to truly be myself in the Gospel—to find freedom and joy in the Good News, not just solemnity.

Through all the years that followed, Ray's spirit of honest freedom never left him. He was relentlessly true, always poking fun, kind, and humorous. We didn't always see eye-to-eye (though I must admit that he was usually right when we did disagree). But never once did I doubt his kindness, his love, or his intention. He called 'em like he saw 'em, and he did it because he cared.

Ray taught me a great lesson. The truth really does set you free.

Not only free from our slavery to sin, but free from our slavery to law. It sets us free to be ourselves, *truly* ourselves, to grow in holiness and happiness.

Have you learned that lesson? Have you surrendered so completely to God that He has been able to give you back the best and most unique and colorful parts of yourself? If you have not found this freedom, ask God for a Ray in your life. Look around for those who clearly are walking in the joy and the freedom of Jesus's Spirit and *imitate them.* Don't copy—*imitate.*

If you've found that freedom, are you sharing it with others? Are you listening to God's voice about whom you can help encourage, empower, and set free? Are you finding a young Luis to mentor, to bring in and adopt as your child as you follow Jesus? You never know how powerfully those choices and relationships can affect the world.

In 1992 my wife, Pat, and I got word that Ray was dying. We dropped everything and went to visit him one last time.

By then it had become obvious that his influence had been one of the turning points in my life. How easily it might not have happened! He could have been so caught up in his own ego, his writing, his successful pastoral career, that he would not have had time to spare for a young kid from a little Argentine town—a kid needy and immature, with nothing to give in return. Most people would have walked right by. But he *saw* me.

When we got to the Stedman house, it was obvious that Ray knew he was dying. I knew that I needed to ask him a couple questions I'd wondered for a long time.

We sat there, Elaine near us, watching on the couch. I said, "Ray, you did so much for me. You poured into my life, you gave me stuff, you took me places. How many others did you help like you did for me over the course of your ministry?"

He looked at Elaine, his old distaste for quoting ego-inducing numbers creeping across his face. Then, in all seriousness, he replied, "Probably about seven hundred."

Seven hundred. I was floored. This man's impact—so much deeper, broader, wider than I had imagined. Praise God.

I waited for another lull in the conversation and looked over again at the man before me who'd given so freely of his time, his attention, his wisdom, his resources, his opinion, his encouragement, his very *self.* I asked, "Then, Ray, why'd you do everything you did for some kid from Argentina?" I asked. "You didn't know anything about me. You just trusted me, brought me here out of the blue."

He looked hard at me with those piercing eyes of his and smiled. "Well, Luis." He cleared his throat. "I just felt the Lord saying, *Bring this kid to the States, Ray.*

"So, I did."

CHAPTER 5

The Secret Fire

Major Ian Thomas and the Secret of the Indwelling Christ

I have been crucified with Christ and I no
longer live, but Christ lives in me. The life I
now live in the body, I live by faith in the Son of
God, who loved me and gave himself for me.

GALATIANS 2:20

That first summer in Palo Alto ended, and I headed north to
Portland, Oregon. The remarkable beauty of the West Coast,
the towering firs and the peaks of the Cascade mountains, formed
an impressive backdrop for studying the Bible.

Ray had urged me to spend a few years at Dallas Theological
Seminary, his alma mater. But four years felt like a lifetime. I was
eager to get to work.

Setting aside their cultural separatism and their rather

self-righteous culture, the church of my youth had done wonders for my training and biblical knowledge. From the time I was a child, Scripture memorization was part of my life. My education at boarding school and St. Albans College had been excellent. I already had experience with preaching, and my preaching had been kindly critiqued by the elders. In my late teens and early twenties, I'd even set up a systematic study of the Bible for myself and had made my way carefully through stacks of classic commentaries. To tell the truth, I felt ready to roar. Still, something was missing. I could feel it. There was passion and purpose in my preparation, but to be honest, I had yet to feel the power that I'd read of in the lives of Wesley, Moody, and others. Perhaps I'd find the missing ingredient that I needed to engage in ministry in earnest.

Multnomah School of the Bible (Multnomah University today) offered a one-year graduate certificate program that I qualified for. Ray recommended Multnomah once he realized that he wasn't going to be able to convince me to spend four years at Dallas, and that one year was likely all the education he'd get into me. The details were worked out, and Luis Palau found himself bound for the intersection of Glisan Street and Eighty-Second Avenue in Portland.

My graduate class had forty-eight students, mostly married and preparing for missions or pastoral work. I was one of only six single men. One spirited Oregon girl in glasses caught my eye, but I wasn't there to do much more than get trained, get my certificate, and get going, so I tried my best to ignore Patricia Scofield. The world needed saving, after all.

Multnomah's campus was unique. It was originally built as a school for the blind. Instead of stairs, students navigated wide-sloping ramps through the old buildings. I lived, ate, and studied on campus, and I settled in to the routine of school well enough. Though my accent was thick, my English was great. We had classes in Bible, theology, journalism, and other necessary disciplines for Christian leaders, and the entire school met together for chapel services three times a week.

Despite my preparation, the stringent program was demanding. What's more, the "missing ingredient"—whatever it was—began to make its absence felt more sharply. I simply couldn't shake the feeling that I was not in the spiritual place I needed to be. The free life that flowed in Ray felt utterly foreign to my soul.

To add insult to that inner injury, I had a professor stuck on a verse that, frankly, had come to annoy me. Dr. George Kehoe would start *every* class session of Spiritual Life (*How do you even claim to teach that in a class?* I thought a bit cynically) by reading Galatians 2:20: "I have been crucified with Christ and I no longer live, but Christ lives in me. The life I now live in the body, I live by faith in the Son of God, who loved me and gave himself for me."

The finality and faith of that verse felt impossible. Paul spoke about that transformation as if it was over and done. Okay. How do I make it happen? And anyway, didn't I have work to do? A calling to pursue? Wasn't the Christian life a struggle to do what God said to do? And just as important, shouldn't we *be* the person God asks us to be?

Those tasks included preaching and teaching quite a bit around the area, even in Multnomah's chapel. All the while, the sense of inner distance grew wider between how I appeared—a promising young international preacher with blue eyes and a winning smile— and how I was—a young man struggling fiercely with arrogance and a sense of self-righteousness. I felt better than those around me, including my professors and the pastors of churches I visited, while still feeling inadequate about being at an American Bible school in the first place. I was falling behind on my reading assignments, which were all in English, and my life was a bit of a complicated mess over those weeks and months.

And I worried. My first semester had been paid for, but what about the second? Let's just say that I wasn't going to be able to pay for it without a bona fide miracle.

Autumn went by, and in Portland that means rain. Not the thunderous drumming rain I was used to in Argentina, which douses you and then lets the sun return. Rather, a steady, slow pour that settled in like it meant to stay until we all got raptured or something. Along with my studies, the rain seemed to highlight my sense that something was missing.

November came. One day I walked to chapel, shivering a little in the misty drizzle that was threatening to become a real Northwest winter. Damp, dreary, and endless.

In the chapel auditorium, I sat in my customary place in the back. I was getting so much Bible in those days that a speaker had to work—hard—to keep my attention. A couple hymns were sung, a prayer, a few announcements made. I was not feeling particularly attentive, though perhaps more attentive than the two nearby students playing chess.

I was glancing over at their game when a man strode up to the podium. He was introduced as Major Ian Thomas. He spoke for precisely twenty-two minutes. And he changed my Christian life.

He had my attention from the beginning. His clipped Oxford accent grabbed my British-educated ear immediately. He was missing half of a finger—a testimony to his distinguished history in combat—which made his strong, elegant gestures just macabre enough to be interesting. He grabbed the attention of the whole room, even the chess players.

I learned later that Major Thomas had a small corner of a London museum dedicated to him, detailing a time that he had single-handedly taken a well-defended Italian mountain from the Nazis, with only a cook backing him up.

He spoke on "the indwelling Christ," and he preached from

the story of Moses and the burning bush. Moses, wandering in the desert and hiding from his people, saw a bush on fire but mysteriously not being consumed, so he investigated. It turned out to be much more than a wild fire, and Moses ended up on holy ground in a life-defining encounter. There at the burning bush Moses met God.

Major Thomas recalled his own experience as a student in medical school, when he was considering missionary work. *I know I'm justified by God's grace*, he thought, *but how do I overcome temptation?* He found the seed of an answer in Romans 5, and the truth blossomed. There *was* a way to live victorious in faith! Being a Christian did not doom you to a lifetime of being Satan's victim. Heart change could come. God had the power to help bring life and belief into alignment. Although the flesh and the old nature were strong, was not Christ stronger still? Wasn't the old nature dead? Hadn't the new come alive?

He told the story of Moses, trained among the Egyptians as a prince, who with one blunder lost hope of delivering his people.

"Maybe this is the dilemma into which you too have fallen," he preached. "You have felt the surge of holy ambition. Your heart has burned within you. You have dreamed dreams and seen visions, but only to awaken again and again to a dull sense of futility, as one who beats the air or builds castles in the sky."[1]

I knew that no matter who else may have been in that room, he was speaking directly to me.

"In his sensitivity to the presence of man," Major Thomas continued, "Moses became strangely insensitive to the presence of God. How easy it is for us to do just that."

"You are not called upon to commit yourself to a need, or to a task, or to a field," he said, with force in every measured syllable.

1 Major Ian Thomas, "Any Old Bush Will Do!," in *The Saving Life of Christ* (Grand Rapids: Zondervan, 1961), 59–70.

"You are called upon to commit yourself to *God*. There are a thousand needs, but you are not committed to these. *You are committed to Christ*."

As he prepared to conclude, he said, "We are tutored in these days to hero worship. In every walk of life, we become fans, and it is not less true in Christian activity. There are those in whose lives there is manifestly evident the mighty unction and power of God. They are transparently genuine. The hand of God is upon them. They speak with an authority that God honors. Lives are transformed, those spiritually dead are raised to life again. Defeated, helpless, useless Christians are transformed into useful vehicles of divine life. Wherever they go, it seems that there is a touch of glory about their path, and we admire them and applaud. But we stand back as though this were to be the monopoly of the few. As though they have a special call upon the grace of God, and as though this were something not for the common run of men. We say in our hearts, 'There is a bush that burns. I would like to be a bush like that, but I am just a heap of ashes.'"

That's me, I thought. I had been trying to move forward in ministry arrogantly, trusting in my education, passion, gifting, personality. But I was called to encounter God first. A genuine experience of His presence needed to be the foundation of my ministry.

"Not I, but Christ in me." I was nothing without Him.

Major Thomas emphasized just how unremarkable a place God chose to inhabit. Was the bush so special? So perfect? So talented? So beautiful? No! "Any old bush will do," he preached, "as long as God is in the bush."

It was God's *presence* that mattered. The power was Christ's, not Luis's. It was only Christ, the mighty and beautiful indwelling resurrected Christ.

To ensure that I didn't miss the point, Major Thomas closed with Galatians 2:20, the same verse my professor repeated every day: "I have been crucified with Christ and I no longer live, but Christ lives in me. The life I now live in the body, I live by faith in the Son of God, who loved me and gave himself for me."

It felt like each word of that verse was being written on my heart in fire. I didn't know whether I wanted to laugh or cry, but I knew I needed to be alone.

He concluded, and I practically ran back to my room. *Lord, I get it*, I prayed. *That's what's been holding me back.* I skipped class without a second thought. I had something more important to do. I returned to my room to pray.

Before this, I had tried my hardest and begged God. But that had been the problem. It was me trying, me begging. I had reached the end of my efforts, knowing that for all my trying, I was not really pleasing God. He wanted more than just my natural gifting or commitment. He wanted *me*. For the first time in my life, I thought that I knew what it might mean to surrender to Him. A prayer in Spanish poured out of me, a prayer of acknowledging and accepting, a prayer of simply asking Him to let my life be about His work through me. I needed to embrace that Christ in me was the hope of glory, and that nothing less than the Sun of Righteousness could shine the light I was looking for in my heart. Saved I had been, but this was a hope for sanctification, and I delighted in it with awestruck, solemn joy.

As I knelt in my sparse room, a sense of overwhelming peace and power began to establish itself in me. I stayed on my knees beside my bunk for an hour and a half. That time marked the great turning point of my spiritual life. It was not the end of growth but the true beginning of it. I did not in any way doubt my salvation before that point, but that moment felt, in its depth and power, like a second conversion. By the time I stood up beside my bunk, I felt like a new man. I felt, from the inside, like a bush on fire.

And nothing would be the same.

Major Thomas's words to us may have just been a good sermon to him. But it changed the trajectory of my inner life. That day was a turning point.

Once I saw the truth of the indwelling Christ, I saw it everywhere. It's all over the New Testament once your eyes are open to it. *Oh, my soul*, you think, *how can I have been reading this and missed it so long?* I think it's because it is not just a matter of discovery but of having it revealed to you. It's a basic transforming truth. You can miss it for years, *thinking* you know what it means but without its power really touching your heart. Even today, its emotional power still gets through to me, even after a lifetime of preaching it. It's just earthshaking.

From then on, there was an unusual blessing on me. I could preach the same messages as before, but they now had a richness and power that they had lacked. Before, my sermons could take a belittling tone. *Are you stupid? Say yes! Why wouldn't you believe this? Why don't you get it?* And people just sat there, staring. Now there was more light, more life, more love, and people responded. There was an immediate, significant difference in my preaching.

Later I found an outline from a sermon that I had preached at a youth conference in Argentina. I laughed when I saw it because it basically had all the principles that Ian Thomas had shared—some of them nearly word for word!—but I had not *experienced* it. I had made an amazing outline, but I hadn't been living in its truth. What a sobering reminder how we can be doing God's work for others with all sincerity and still fail to understand how it applies to our own lives. Preaching it doesn't mean you experience it.

I gradually realized that I had found the "union and communion" that Hudson Taylor had written so poignantly about. Moody called it the "anointing" and spoke freely about his own experience of shutting himself up in a friend's room in New York, praying like I had, and emerging a different preacher, a different man.

This truth, what Major Thomas called "the indwelling Christ," infused fresh life into my faith. Belief was not just intellectual or practical. It felt like it was woven into me. My inner state quietly began to shift. I began to experience a kind of peace that I recognized in Ray but simply hadn't felt before. Christ was living—*in me!* It was real and simple, and it transformed my choices, my way of life. I understood deeply why the Gospel is Good News. It wasn't just about getting converted; it was about *living as converted.* It wasn't flashy; it was glorious. It wasn't show business or Hollywood fakery; it was reality. I wasn't putting on an act. I didn't have to. This was real whether I was preaching from a stage or simply walking through the neighborhoods in Portland.

I had passed through a great spiritual crossroads—one that I didn't know I had been standing at until it was behind me. As I continued to speak and teach as invitations came in, I began to craft a statement to remind me of the truth that had confronted me so meaningfully.

I wrote the following in my Bible on the blank page facing the beginning of the Old Testament. They are written in different inks, from pens throughout the years—black, red, green, blue:

I am here by God's appointment.

God is being glorified. He is here in me. God is here. Literally.

I know His will and His words. Fire and power!

Confidence.

Decision by faith—call people to a decision and expect them to come.

God is speaking. An encounter with God by the soul through the Word.

Expectancy: The Holy Spirit is at work, right here, right now. He promised.

Humility—nothing of myself. Only Him.

Compassion! Eternal destinies are at stake.

Revival—awakening for believers.

Harvest—conquer lost masses.

Urgency!

Drama—Redemption is at work in lives for eternity.

Decisions!

For all my outward confidence, I still frequently got nervous as I prepared to preach. Perhaps the service would be starting late; or the crowd would be restless, making me wonder if they'd even be listening; or the musicians would be off key, annoying my inner desire to have everything perfect as I began.

I had been preaching and working from my own strength, and it was never enough. Now I was resting in God's presence and promises. And He was enough. It was tremendous rest.

Little did I know then how deeply I would need to work from that place of rest in the years to come.

It takes a blend of peace and courage that can only come from beyond you to navigate certain tough situations. In the sixties and seventies, as my ministry was taking me farther into difficult regions of Latin America, this became especially apparent in my interactions with Communists, particularly atheistic Marxists and

Leninists. These years were particularly hot ones for being in the middle of the Cold War, and tensions were high in several politically unstable nations.

In many of these nations, the choice was not only between the status-quo government and revolution but also between fresh ideologies.

Castro, whose revolution had taken Cuba in 1959, goaded me into my fierce opposition of Marxism. "The first thing we do is kill all the lawyers," one communist leader was quoted as saying. "Second, we kill the priests and pastors." Considering those comments, I felt that I had the freedom to speak against Marxism, so I did. One of my most well-known radio sermons was broadcast out of Costa Rica and featured a clever pun in its title: *Cristo o Castro?* ("Christ or Castro?"). That was the choice many were forced to make. They could turn to the cyclical violence of bloody revolution, or they could turn to the blood of Jesus, who could change the heart of a nation, beginning with *us*.

As you might imagine, most Communist leaders did not appreciate my sermon. In fact, they hated it. And they hated me. This made certain places a bit dicey to preach in.

I later learned (from a very reliable source) that a transcript of my sermon was read and filed away by every Marxist party in Latin America. I am sure that things were going on around me that I had no idea of. I do not know the extent to which God protected me, but I can tell you that it gave me the creeps when one high-ranking secretary of the Communist Party in Ecuador told me, as she puffed on a cigarette, "Palau, from the moment you landed in our country, we knew exactly where you were at every given moment, recorded everything you said, knew the hotel you stayed in, who drove you there, and the whole story."

I was glad that I didn't learn that until later. Not knowing the extent of the Communist Party's interest in me, and full of passion to preach about people's true freedom, I used to go after the Communists publicly. I scheduled speeches and preached at universities where I'd be met by huge groups of Marxist activists. I used to really tangle in those days. When you're young, you like a good fight, you know? We'd get into outright shouting matches. It was youthful passion, but the methods were much more me than the indwelling Christ, I'm afraid, and it didn't produce much.

At one university in South America, I got into a particularly heated encounter. The handful of believers in the crowd had snuck in, acting like they didn't know who I was for their own safety. I could feel that the crowd was hostile. Almost all of the three thousand students in attendance were Communists or Communist sympathizers. I started to give my speech, when a Communist leader leapt up on stage and grabbed the mic from me.

"Hey, hey, hey," I said, "I'm here. You can speak after. It's my turn now, man."

"To h—with you," he replied, and that was the least of his curses. He went on and on, getting quite imaginative in his flowery descriptions of me and Christianity.

Finally, I interrupted his tirade, shouting back, "Fine, if you're going to do this, I'm leaving! Have fun, buddy."

"You're not going to speak here," he shouted.

"Fine. See you!" I replied, and I walked out. As I left, I kept trying to shake hands with people, but nobody would shake my hand. I started looking people in the eyes and asking them "What are you afraid of? I've got no weapons!" The whole atmosphere felt tense, like a bomb was about to go off, but I returned to my hotel without incident.

The next day, the leader of the Marxist party of the university called me up and invited me to his house to eat. A fine meal was prepared. We sat together, and I started eating.

At one point, he looked me dead in the eyes. "How did you

have the guts to come here?" he asked quietly, regarding me with a strange look. "I could have poisoned you."

I finished chewing (the food was really quite good) and swallowed. "Yeah, you could have poisoned me," I said. "But on the other hand, if He'd wanted to, God could have poisoned you."

What can you do but laugh at that point? I was not dead. Neither was he. We might as well try to become friends. And with that as our introduction, we really did. We discussed many topics at the table that day. We left with neither of us having shifted our opinions. But we had eaten together, and neither of us were the worse for it, praise God.

Our work was never politically focused. But it did have political and social implications. When people come to heartfelt faith that governs their lives, and they gather in churches, aside from the spiritual implications (which are the most vital, of course), they begin to live differently. The vacuum of values and care for one's neighbors that allows corruption and cruelty to flourish begins to fill with something new and positive. If the heart change is real, the social change will be too. Nominal religion may indeed be the "opium of the people," as Karl Marx famously said. It numbs them. It can be used to bolster the corrupt by spiritualizing injustice or glossing over oppression. The truth can be twisted to say almost anything in the name of God. But true Christianity wakes you up. It changes the world, beginning with your heart.

As a result, our work truly opposed the spread of destructive ideologies of the twentieth century. It equally challenged the corrupted and unfair forces of the status-quo that moved many toward violent regimes in the first place. Christ's love comes to rule both the rulers and their rebels.

Years later, an influential pastor went to Cuba and met with the aging Fidel Castro. At my request, I asked him to try to convince the leader to let me come to Cuba and preach. In their meeting, the pastor said, "There's a Latin preacher that would love to come to Cuba and speak to the people. He promises that he will only preach the Gospel, not attack the government."

"Who is he?" Castro asked.

"Luis Palau," said my friend.

"Luis Palau!" Castro shouted to my friend. "Sure, he can come. He can fly in, hop straight in a taxi, drive around the airport, and get right back out of here!"

Still angry after all that time. All because I had insisted that Jesus leads the only revolution that works.

As the years passed, I gradually learned that the mystery of the indwelling Christ did not mean that fiery Luis was gone. Quite the opposite. At the best of times, God's Spirit used my feisty side to carry me through when I needed to tell the truth with some spice in it.

One God, the Trinity, chooses to dwell in us. The Spirit of Jesus is in us—what a glorious mystery!

It is a grave mistake to think that God wishes to use only the pretty, the privileged, the strong, the healthy, and the favored. No, He can use *any* of us. Is not His glory shown even more brightly when it is the weak, the poor, the clumsy, and the awkward who carry His message forward with power? It is in weakness that we grow in strength.

That power has carried me throughout my ministry. But do not mistake it for mine. It is His. I have not always walked in His power as single-mindedly as I should. I have often fallen back to rest on my own gifting or strength. I have often wished that I was more like my heroes of the faith, who genuinely seemed to have had a clarity and purity to their walk with Christ that helped their efforts. I have often wished I was more defined by the "Christ" of "Christ in me" than the "me."

Truly understanding "Christ in me" is a lesson that every Christian must learn for themselves. You can read it, know it, and even preach it, but if it has not entered your *heart* through desperation and surrender, then you do not have it. It is the great secret of Christianity.

Do you have that secret? Have you ever so experienced the Spirit of Jesus that His life has inexplicably, undeniably become yours? Have you tasted—even if only for a fleeting moment—what it means to walk in the joyous victory that is "Christ in you, the hope of glory"?

If not, go to Him. Cry out to Him. Fully surrender to Him. Know the depth of His love for you. He wants you to live in peace, power, and victory. Stop concentrating on others as heroes of the faith, and understand that *you* have access to the same power and depth that you admire in those you have held up.

There is another side to this, though, one that only comes with age. The life of the indwelling Christ is all too easy to think of as something that happened "back then." My life in 1960 was fine. But what about now? Where is my heart today?

Where are you today with Christ? Are you dwelling in true union and communion with Him? Is your life characterized by His victory and fire or by the ashes of defeat? Do you truly believe that He is ready to give you the purity of purpose and power that you admire in the great Christians you have known? He is.

If God could do that for young Luis Palau on a cold November morning, I guarantee that He can do it for you.

Right now.

Ask Him!

CHAPTER 6

Living Sacrifice

My Wife, Patricia Scofield de Palau

> I did not run or labor in vain. But even if I am
> being poured out like a drink offering on the
> sacrifice and service coming from your faith, I
> am glad and rejoice.
>
> PHILIPPIANS 2:16–17

My discovery of the indwelling Christ happened about the same time as an equally unexpected development in my heart. I met someone.

Patricia Scofield was another student in the one-year graduate program. I can't remember where she was the first time I saw her. Maybe she was simply walking through the library, or perhaps she was at the center of a group of grad students. But she caught my eye. You couldn't help but notice her. She was freewheeling, confident, smart, pretty, and she had a backbone of grit and resolve that I immediately admired. She was, in a word, *attractive*.

Her quick wit and razor-sharp intelligence were formidable. We had nearly every class together. In class and out, she had a bulldog-like tenacity and an attention for theological detail and nuance, balanced with real care for the well-being of others. She was the kind of fellow student that everyone listened to. When she said something, you knew that it was going to be good—and probably a little challenging!

I tried to mask my feelings at first, with roundabout inner monologues like *Hmm. That Pat is kind of nice, I guess.* I just happened to bump into her everywhere. She lived off campus in a rented room in the home of a little old Christian lady. Somehow I kept turning up—in the library, on walks in between buildings, in lingering conversations after class. She'd go someplace. Then I always seemed to show up.

I must admit it wasn't all accidental. From my dorm window, I could see Pat coming up the sidewalk from her house off campus. I always timed it so I'd happen to step out just when she was in front of the building. What a coincidence! And the coincidences just kept getting more . . . coincidental.

I found out later that others started noticing my growing attention more than I allowed myself to. "Hey, Pat, do you notice that Luis always seems to show up when you're around?" her friends began to tease her. "We think he's following you." And it wasn't too many weeks before I had to admit it: I was interested. *Really* interested.

Those "accidental" meetings started becoming intentional. We began to spend time together on purpose. We weren't dating in the official sense, but at the get-togethers and parties of the grad program, we always had our eyes on each other. I soon realized that I did not simply come to Portland to learn; I came to meet Pat. By the end of our Christmas break, we'd begun a serious relationship. Our school had fire escapes that were giant slides—for the blind, remember?—and I'd use those to slide out and visit Pat any chance I could get.

As I got to know her, she only got more interesting. She was a local girl. She grew up on the other side of the West Hills of Portland, out in the beautiful farm country of the Willamette Valley. She was from a place called Cedar Mill, and little did I know then how well I'd get to know that quaint name.

Pat came from a ministry family. Her grandparents founded Cedar Mill Bible Church, and her dad was an elder there. She had gotten her undergraduate degree from Seattle Pacific University and was now at Multnomah in preparation for missions work. She'd felt drawn to missions ever since she was a girl at a missions conference at her home church. She was committed to it. We shared the view that life was about proclaiming the Good News. Where did she want to go? She wasn't sure yet, but perhaps Taiwan or somewhere else in Asia.

Our growing relationship prompted some inner wrestling. I hadn't come to the States looking for a girlfriend or a wife. I came to learn and get going. I hadn't planned on meeting Pat.

I would walk her from campus to her house, which sat exactly fifty-two yards away—what you might call a short-distance relationship. On those walks, we talked about theology, dreamed about missions, and analyzed what our professors had been lecturing on. Things moved fast after those short walks began. I realized that I was quickly becoming unable to picture my future without Pat in it.

What my initial marriage proposal lacked in romantic acumen, it made up for in simple honesty about our calling. We were in the middle of campus by a tree with a swing. We were talking about the mission field, pondering where our callings might take us. "Would you, um"—I hesitated—"Ever consider coming to Latin America?" Real subtle, Palau! Subtle and *very* obscure.

"Sure, I'd consider it," she said meaningfully. And characteristic of the marriage that followed, we understood precisely what the other had just said.

We went to meet her folks. Her father was rather bashful. He told Pat's mother to tell Pat, "If he wants to marry her, I'm okay with it, but don't come and ask me! Just tell him not to ask for her hand because I don't know how to deal with that." I did it anyway. He managed to give his consent in person. Then I gave him a hug, and he stiffened up, for Americans didn't hug each other in those days—especially not men. He probably wondered what kind of crazy Latin was carrying off his daughter!

By Easter it was decided. I officially proposed on that holiday in Pat's family's backyard. I gave her a ring and a corsage, and we had some formal photos taken. It was a done deal! There I was, in the States for less than a year, engaged to be married.

We wed on August 5, 1961, at Cedar Mill Bible Church. We honeymooned on the rugged and beautiful coast of Oregon and then spent a week at a cottage in Lake Tahoe, California, loaned to us by a dear friend. And just like that, I was married to the most remarkable woman in the world.

We graduated from the program at Multnomah together and immediately began training with Overseas Crusades. It was 1961, and Pat and I went to complete a missionary internship in Detroit supervised by a man named Fred Renich.

I was still growing in my understanding of what it meant to minister through the power of the indwelling Christ, and a piece of advice that Fred gave me put it into remarkably practical terms. "Before your feet hit the floor in the morning," Fred said, "say to yourself, *Today I'm going to face temptations I don't know how to handle, questions I don't know how to answer, opportunities to witness I will not see, needs I cannot meet, problems I cannot solve. But You are here in me. You will find a way."* That affirmation became a daily reminder of His presence. I have been faced with those temptations, questions, opportunities, needs, and problems countless times. If I had not done my best to surrender in this way, I don't know where I'd be.

And as He tends to do, the Lord used Fred to teach me just how far I had to go. Understanding is one thing; living it is another. And I was about to be humbled. Considerably.

In Detroit, Pat and I rented a small upstairs room in the home of an old woman. The local church that we were assigned to as trainees had put us in touch with her. I'm not quite sure the correct terminology to use these days, but she was . . . odd. Though we were paying for the room, she refused adamantly to give us a key to it, meaning that we couldn't lock our door.

We were a young couple, just married. As you can imagine, privacy was more than a convenience. We *needed* it. This little old lady would walk in with a plate of cookies, opening our door without so much as a knock. She was silent like a cat until *there she was.* I got really miffed.

"Madam," I said, "we're paying for this room. We need a key for it." No matter what I said, she wouldn't give it to us. Furious, I decided to take some action, but instead of going to Fred, my local supervisor, I went over his head, straight to our sending mission. I was rash. "If I don't get the key from this woman," I wrote, "I'm quitting and heading back West."

The mission acted instantly. They called Fred and, in no uncertain terms, asked him how he was supervising us when a basic need wasn't being handled. Fred called me in for a conversation. "Luis," he said, "I hear that you're having problems with your landlady. I just found out." My heart sank as I realized what was happening. "Do you know how I found out? Your boss in OC called me up. He was really put off. I had to tell him that I had no idea this was going on. And let me tell you, he laid into me."

He paused for a minute. "Why didn't you just come to me? Do you know how bad this makes me look? It makes me seem careless, like a terrible supervisor. But I was never given a chance to fix it because you didn't tell me."

I began to apologize. I would have loved for the conversation to end right there, but it didn't. Fred quickly pointed out that this wasn't an isolated incident. It was an opportunity to consider my fiery and dangerous temperament.

"You're aggressive, Luis," he said. "You're goal conscious and know exactly what you want, and you are going to get it, no matter what. But look back, even now at twenty-five, and you'll see that you are beginning to leave corpses behind you—people you've hurt as you move along. You haven't even really begun to lead anything. You're on a dangerous trajectory. Keep this up and you are going to destroy people in the name of ministry. If you don't do some radical soul-searching and change, you are setting yourself up to get all your goals and crush lives in the process."

I retreated to the little upstairs room that started the whole mess. Was *this* the power of the indwelling Christ that I'd been so excited about? *I'm a hypocrite*, I thought. *I'm going to destroy people. Maybe I already have.*

I prayed hard and began listing all the people that I might have hurt—however unintentionally. Little things that I had dismissed suddenly seemed like a big deal with Fred's words ringing in my ears. How had my loud, aggressive tone—which I was in the habit of using—shoved others aside or buried their ideas? Over the next several days, I wrote notes to many of the people I suspected I'd hurt somehow, and I asked for their forgiveness. Many replied saying that they hadn't felt that way at all, which was reassuring, but it didn't lessen the purifying nature of the experience. Writing those notes was a way of letting the weight of my words and actions sink in, of considering how Christ in me really ought to relate to those around me.

In that eye-opening moment with Fred Renich, one of the great themes of my life with Pat stands out. While it would be impossible for me to boil down our relationship to a single lesson that she taught me, she has absolutely exemplified what it means to be a living sacrifice. Pat's example of pouring herself out was eye opening and at the very heart of our ministry.

The fact that her sacrifice was combined with such strength of character made it even more incredible. Pat is gifted beyond words. Hers was not a passive, naïve, or weak sacrifice. It was chosen, committed to, and followed through with elegance. She made what would crush others look nearly effortless.

Soon after Detroit, our missionary days began. To tell the story of those years would take another whole book. Early on, I was frustrated. I knew my call: mass evangelism in big cities (more on that call later). Our organization made few promises and concessions in that direction, but they still demanded that I pour most of my time into little things at home. It felt like the mission was not opening opportunities fast enough.

As Pat says today, that frustration was the best thing that could have happened to us. The leaders saw that they needed to hold me back for my own good. They must have thought, *Luis needs to be put in his place or he's going to get out of control.* But they saw something I didn't see. As much as it frustrated me at the time, I know that for a man of my drive and personality, too much too soon in ministry can doom him, either through failure (which is bad) or by success (which can be worse). Looking back, I see Pat's pure and selfless wisdom reflected in understanding what was really happening. Those years helped Pat's service take on the deep meaning that it did. She saw from the beginning that it wasn't just about our work. We were also the ones being worked on.

Our work in those years had us living in Latin America: Costa Rica, Colombia, and Mexico. All those places were dangerous in those days, especially for an American woman and her blond little kids who stood out no matter how discreet they were. We experienced break-ins and thievery in one capital city that made my heart sink as a husband and father. I was already traveling for extended periods of time: three-to five-week stretches. It was getting harder and harder to leave them, not only because of my desire to be with them but also because I was worried. It was getting difficult to shake the constant awareness that *anything* could be happening back at home—right at that moment—and it became too much.

Pat deeply wanted to be in the field. She wanted to live among the people and to minister in one place for a lifetime. Even though we made the decision to return to and plant our home base in Oregon, as it became apparent that my mass evangelism ministry was the core of our calling, she was never fully satisfied. She had to sacrifice what she'd long felt called to—overseas missions. It was hard.

But we took that missionary spirit with us. I laugh when people try to lump me in with the so-called evangelists who are only in their "ministry" for the money they can con out of people. If only those people saw how we live! We have never lacked anything we needed, and we have had many extras. But we have never had a lavish lifestyle.

When we moved recently, it was telling to see what kind of things were being packed into boxes: no luxuries (at least not by American standards), too many books, a few decorations, clothes, and many photos (for pictures become more valuable as you get older, connecting you to the memories and feelings of days long past).

Pat tried to give some of our extra stuff away to the Salvation Army as we were moving. They turned us down! When a thrift store says, "Thanks, but no thanks," I guess you haven't lost that missionary spirit.

The point is winning people. Who cares about jewelry? Who cares about the stuff that people spend money on? People give their lives to so much foolishness, so many distractions. Pat and I would not change a thing.

Servanthood is not in vogue right now. Was it ever? It's not fashionable to pour out your life, interests, time, and energy for the sake of others. Having a servant's attitude is seen as a weakness, like you're not living up to your potential. Yet servanthood requires incredible strength. A servant realizes the unimaginable potential in God's kingdom. Remember what Jesus taught? "The greatest among you will be your servant. For those who exalt themselves will be humbled, and those who humble themselves will be exalted" (Matthew 23:11–12).

What a stirring truth! The self-sacrifice of a servant unlocks God's exaltation and honor. The degree to which we serve is the degree to which we are great in God's eyes.

I ask myself, as my life draws to a close, how great I am in God's eyes. Am I quick to serve in the humble, invisible ways that show our true heart as Pat, "the wife of my youth" does? Am I willing to become less so that others can become greater? Am I willing to lay aside my desires, to put others' needs before my own and simply *give*? It is harder for me than I'd like to admit.

How about for you? Have you thanked God for the people in your life who have poured themselves out for your benefit? He has provided for you through them. Praise Him for it!

Pat often says that one of the greatest sins we commit is taking another person for granted. How many times have I come close to doing that! But now, seeing her influence as one of the great and abiding forces in my life, there is no way that I can do that.

My wife has poured out her love, her wisdom, her humor, and her intelligence. She has given her time, her tears, her energy, her sense of safety and security. She laid down her dream of a life overseas to better serve our sons and give me the freedom to travel. On every stage I have ever stood upon, her spirit has been standing beside me. On every radio broadcast, every television show, every *everything*, she has made her influence felt. My life, the lives of our sons, and the life of this world is immeasurably richer because of her. My only regret is that I did not honor her more publicly from the beginning, not only as a wife and mother—that I always did— but as a partner in the work of evangelism. Her influence on me is incalculable.

Pat's sense of humor is rather earthy, like her general view of life. She is a realist, but she's also easier going on some things than I am. Inside, I'm still an old fundamentalist, but she helps me loosen up and helps me see how love and laughter and sports are part of living in the Good News. Life in Christ should be a joyful life! We can't just preach that. We must live it.

She thinks her own thoughts, makes up her own mind, and I love her for it. For certain sins that Christians tend to shake our fingers at enthusiastically, she'll ask one of those terribly uncomfortable questions that make you stop and think. "If it was your son or daughter, would you say that?" She sticks up for everyone, for their human dignity and their value in the eyes of God, no matter what. Maybe she has that Oregon pioneer spirit—adaptable, loyal, strong.

Committed.

Pat and I have been married for fifty-seven years. When you add up all the time I have spent traveling during our marriage, Pat and I have spent a cumulative *fifteen years* of our marriage apart. That is just how it was. I couldn't preach to the masses from my couch. I had to travel. Evangelists like me hit the road. We must, or we would be different than we are.

My work made profound demands on Pat, to whom fell the responsibility of caring for our sons.

All of this, Pat did gladly for the kingdom. She is not the kind of person to talk about it. She is not the kind to make grandiose statements or draw attention to herself. The words of 2 Corinthians 5:14–15 perfectly depict her lifestyle's foundation:

> For Christ's love compels us, because we are convinced that one died for all, and therefore all died. And he died for all, that those who live should no longer live for themselves but for him who died for them and was raised again.

Sometimes I overhear Pat talking to others about ministry past and present, and it is gratifying. She really believed in what we were doing—and still does. This sacrifice was inspired by more than simply a sense of wifely duty or force of habit. Pat's honesty and integrity helped make her life as much of a missionary story as any in Christian history. She gave herself up as a living sacrifice for the sake of the Gospel. She believed. She committed. To this day, she claims it wasn't a big deal. Give me a break! It *was* a big deal. Pat, your work shaped our boys, shaped our ministry. For many, your work helped shape *eternity*.

Even though she had opportunities to teach, speak, write, and strategize, Pat was usually a quiet witness. We recognized that we were a team, each one doing a role that, because of our different personalities and giftings, the other could not do. It inspired me that I could leave my family for long stretches without feeling totally guilty. I did feel guilty sometimes, on top of the natural sadness of being separated from Pat and the boys. I don't think I would have been a good husband and father if I did not have any guilt. Now that period of life is over, and I ask myself if I would change it. Not really. It makes me emotional to say.

Pat has always been laser-focused on our calling. She was never passive and never gave up, no matter the challenge. Her missionary heart, her ability to help me hone my messages—she has been indispensable. She is a bulldog for the Gospel.

We often have talked about how we wished we could be together more. But the whole point of our lives was winning people to Christ. That is what we worked for together. Even when we were thousands of miles apart, we were working side-by-side. We did different tasks, but we shared a goal. Most importantly, we shared a Master. From the beginning, we have lived to lead as many people as possible to Christ. Everything else is good but secondary.

Pat is loath to speak about herself, never wanting to brag or be self-aggrandizing. Pat's spirit of committed servanthood arises from the depth of her trust in God. From deep and sincere faith comes the courage to truly serve with your life—yes, even to risk your life for service. I could tell countless stories to illustrate this, but I'll share only two.

In Scotland in 1980, on the prolonged campaign through the United Kingdom that would eventually take us to Mission to London, Pat joined me for about a week. She seemed somber and preoccupied. I began racking my mind, wondering what I could have done to upset her. (We husbands always seem to think it's about *us*, don't we?) I had been gone about seven weeks, after all.

Had I done something? Perhaps I hadn't written enough? Forgotten something important?

Finally, I just asked it. "Hey, what's going on?"

"Come touch here," she said, taking my hand and pressing it to her breast. "A lump, Luis." It definitely was. "I think it's serious," she said.

We got back to the States the following Monday. By Thursday, the doctor's biopsy confirmed that it was cancer.

When the doctor told us the news, the doctor stepped out to give us a minute. I tried my hardest to reassure myself by reassuring her. "You'll be fine," I told her.

"No," she said, "this is the end."

Her certainty took me aback. I had known loss. The pain of losing my father suddenly welled up in my heart, and I did not even want to *begin* considering that for my beloved. "No," I replied immediately. "No, no. God is going to heal you."

The doctor returned with our next steps. Pat was to go into the hospital on Sunday for a Monday surgery. The fast pace alone should tell you how seriously they were taking this.

We returned home from the doctor to our little split-level house on Jody Street in Beaverton. I felt utterly spent, stunned. Though my faith in God didn't waver in the least, it felt like the air had been punched out of me. My wife? *Cancer?*

I went straight to the basement to be alone. I started to weep, to really cry, hard, with big, racking sobs. Love made the tears come like that—the love that suddenly realizes just how fragile the person it loves is. In the blur of tears, all that I could think of was how Pat had wanted to take a trip to Hawaii recently, and I'd shot the idea down, feeling a bit stingy. *Luis, you swine!* I thought. *Why didn't you just take her? Now it's probably too late.*

In the midst of my grief, I began to hear music. It came down into the basement through the floor above, a piano, starting softly on a familiar melody and slowly gaining volume. The notes came with growing confidence, and then a voice rising to accompany it. Pat was playing one of the old hymns and singing with strength in her voice:

> *Under His wings I am safely abiding,*
> *Though the night deepens and tempests are wild.*
> *Still I can trust Him, I know He will keep me,*
> *He has redeemed me and I am His child.*

Her voice swelled with faith. It overwhelmed me. On this occasion, when she could have very well just heard her death sentence, she chose to return home and worship. What beautiful faith. What total trust. That's what Jesus Christ our Lord brings into our life—not ease but the strength to bear the difficulty.

The other story to illustrate Pat's complete servanthood and sacrifice is more humorous but no less poignant.

While we were missionaries in Cali, Colombia, I returned home after a trip of several weeks. Pat and I decided to take a short vacation in Bogotá, the capital. We left the kids with a couple maids—which, in hindsight, we *never* should have done. They were nice enough, Christian girls from the country. They loved the Lord and were happy to be living with missionaries, but to leave our twins with them? What a responsibility! Especially since the blond boys stood out so much in the city, and violence and kidnappings never seemed to happen *quite* far enough away.

Our exhausted young-parent minds made the decision. Pat and I kissed our little ones, then hopped in a taxi for the Cali airport, and thence to Bogotá.

She claims to this day that what I'm about to tell you never happened. (Don't listen to her. She said it!) But on the ride in the taxi, we passed a pasture, and she turned to me and said, "Ooooh! Lookie! Horsies!"

"Pat," I replied, "the boys aren't here."

Sure, it's funny, but isn't it also an incredible example of service? She was giving up so much of her own hopes and dreams to serve our boys, and even when she wasn't with them, her immediate reaction was to speak as though they were. If that is not Christlike, I do not know what is. To be with your children in the middle of a sometimes violent foreign land, to spend so much time, so much energy, so much of yourself on them that you, as intelligent and *brilliant* as you are, fall into the habit of speaking on a toddler's level? That is love. That is commitment. That is being a living sacrifice like Jesus Himself. Although I chuckle at the story, I wonder how many of us have so totally emptied ourselves for others. A good mother's love is the definition of self-giving service.

Pat and I were in Paraguay in 2014. While we were in Asunción, the capital, we met the daughter of some German missionaries. She was a lawyer, working on behalf of the children of a small community of the Chaco. As she talked about her home and work, Pat's missionary spirit was stirred.

For the past fifty years, I had been broadcast on a Christian radio station that reached all the way out to the five tribal areas. The people thought of me as their best friend! They had been asking for years for me to come and preach, but I had never been able to prioritize it. Pat, ever with an eye for those who might be overlooked, would have none of that after meeting the missionaries' daughter. "I'm going for a visit to El Chaco with you or without you," she said. And that sealed it.

Part of what had held us back in the past had been the logistics. Accessing the area was tough. It was in the middle of nowhere. They wanted to find an auditorium to travel to for the campaign, but our team members in Paraguay and Argentina wanted to do it right. "We're going to go to them," we decided.

So we went. About five tribal groups were represented in the town of about seven thousand (which is a big city way out there). The tribes had been joined for years by old-fashioned German and Russian Mennonites. A large arch leading into the town commemorated the Mennonites' arrival, and a big platform for preaching stood right there in the symbolic heart of the community.

The campaign was not easy, but it was fantastic. The highlight of it for me, though, was when Pat, the catalyst for the whole event, took the stage.

They wanted to hear her. She got up to share her testimony, and I joined her as her backup and to help translate. But she never said a word in English! She spoke simply but eloquently in Spanish, telling her story. When it was over, I simply chuckled. "Thank you very much, Mrs. Palau!"

How wonderful it felt to stand by her side in a place we would not have gone without her vision and to see souls saved as a result.

When the apostle Paul wrote that he was "being poured out" for the church, what did that mean? It meant that his very life was being spent on behalf of others. It meant that his best was being given away.

Not all sacrifice is Christlike though. Sometimes service can still be about ourselves. Sometimes we need to be needed. Sometimes we confuse being helpful with pouring ourselves out. There is no recipe for what makes sacrifice truly Christlike. But ask yourself this: *Am I learning how to sacrifice by imitating Jesus?* He is our model, our pattern. He is the image that we are called by God the Father to emulate. Whether we are international preachers or stay-at-home parents, the call is the same. Serve others like Christ did, giving your life for others.

Pat says that there were moments when her role and mine did not seem "fair." But she immediately follows it with this sentence, in the kind of tone that she uses when her bulldog conviction is coming to the surface: "But *fair* is not a good word. Of course it is not fair. Nothing is. Grace is the antithesis of fair. We aren't keeping score in this marriage or this ministry." Pat's Christlike attitude shows me the Gospel here in my own home. She humbles me and forces me to put things in perspective. If we are not going to do what is necessary to bring the Gospel to those who need it, then who will? Somebody must "sacrifice."

"Life *is* fair in the long view," she continues. "God knows, and He always does what is right."

Yes, He does. Through people like Pat who have taught me about Christ's self-giving spirit of service, God is changing the world one heart at a time.

CHAPTER 7

Under the Mighty Hand

The Humility of Billy Graham

Humble yourselves therefore under the mighty
hand of God, that he may exalt you in due time.

1 PETER 5:6 KJV

I first heard the voice late one night when the rest of the house
was asleep.

It was 1950. I was sixteen or so, staying overnight with my aunt
and uncle.

It was past midnight, but in good Argentine fashion (we're night
owls), I wasn't the least bit sleepy. To pass the time, I laid down on
the floor and clicked on the shortwave radio. Keeping the volume
on the absolute minimum, I moved the dial. Music crackled, and
voices faded in and out until, with a little thrill, I heard a man's
voice speaking English.

Though the volume was only a whisper, I could tell that the voice was resonant, confident, and booming. He had a preacher's voice—and a good one at that. I moved my ear closer to the radio. The man was shouting out the conclusion of a sermon. His presentation of the Gospel fairly rang with faith, and something in my heart awoke as I heard it. The man concluded, prayed passionately, and then a rich, manly voice swelled into an old hymn:

> *Out of my bondage, sorrow, and night,*
> *Jesus, I come, Jesus, I come;*
> *Into thy freedom, gladness, and light,*
> *Jesus, I come to thee.*

I had given my life to the Lord at age twelve while sitting on a fallen log on that rainy night at summer camp. But I wasn't feeling particularly close to Him. In fact, quite the opposite. I attended a Bible study at school, which was fine, but I went for the tea and treats as much as anything. At that all-boys school, mockery of pretty much anything, especially faith, was rewarded with laughter. My conscience particularly haunted me for failing to stand up when a couple friends were picked on and then beaten up for their faith. (One of those bullied boys, David Leake, later became the Anglican bishop of Northern Argentina.) I really wanted to defend them, but I didn't—so I felt like a coward. Skinny as I was, I couldn't have done much, but I at least could have stood with them and taken a smack or two in the gut.

Lately I had been joining the rest of my companions in their joking, feeling that it was wrong but caring more about their affirmation than about living for Jesus. One day, after a Bible study, I forgot my Bible on the street car. In a clear expression of where my heart was at, I didn't even try to retrieve it.

The quiet sermon nailed me, elegantly showing my arrogance.

Lord, I'm coming home, I felt, as the hymn came quietly out of the radio. The Lord and I reconciled—and it was listening to the conclusion of Billy Graham's message that prompted it. *You've been listening to Billy Graham,* the radio crackled, followed by Cliff Barrows signing off: "If you want to write, 'Billy Graham, Minneapolis, Minnesota,' is all the address you need." I later learned that I'd tuned in to a missionary radio station, HCJB, "The Voice of the Andes," broadcasting from Ecuador, for the end of *The Hour of Decision.*

That was my first encounter with Mr. Graham. It was a bit one-sided but profound nonetheless.

Not long afterward, several things happened. There were so few evangelical believers in Argentina in those days that when somebody came from overseas to evangelize, it was a big event. A businessman, a German who'd fled the Nazis after helping to protect the persecuted Jews, was bringing a film about Martin Luther that was banned by the local religious authorities for being Protestant and heretical. So there was a bit of an air of secrecy about it, which piqued my interest even more.

The German businessman gave me a book, *Revival in Our Time.* It was the story of Billy Graham in Los Angeles, plus Portland and Boston, and included six of his sermons. It named some of Billy's more notable converts, including Louis Zamperini, a former Olympic runner and prisoner of war (recently featured in the best-selling book and movie *Unbroken*). The book may have essentially been publicity, but for me it was explosive, exciting, and fresh.

I was about nineteen. I had begun dreaming of the big cities, of preaching and evangelizing the masses. And here was a man who was doing precisely that! I hadn't heard about his ministry but was already seeing that if I wanted to reach a whole city, I couldn't just sit in a little church of 130 people. How would we impact the nearly one *million* people of Córdoba? It wouldn't happen in our sanctuary. It wouldn't really happen with street preaching. We needed to dream bigger. And Billy's dreams were a step ahead.

I began thinking about strategy. The poor readily listen to the Gospel because it is Good News for them. The rich seem to have a harder time—think about what the Bible says to the rich of this world. But the rich often have social influence. The wealthy tend to sneer at you and decide whether they'll listen to you based on things that don't ultimately matter: pedigree, education, net worth.

Fortunately, I was able to hobnob with the children of the wealthy. I had come from money, had gone to the right schools, and was bilingual. I loved those rich kids. But the Gospel had a hard time getting through to their families, and the reputation of evangelicals as a small group of ignorant, gullible, backwards people got in the way.

In those days, having a telephone was a big deal. Only those doing alright financially could afford a phone. And phone books, listing the numbers of everyone in the city, were gold mines of names and addresses. As part of our strategy to reach the upper classes, we decided to use a magazine, *La Voz*, that I worked part time for, and mail it to all the names in the phone book. With the help of a dynamic American writer living in Argentina, the magazine turned out well, and we were proud of what we mailed out. It was well written, looked good, and presented our faith as something more than a sect for hopeless, impoverished people. The Gospel is that—hope for the poor—but it is more than that too. The Gospel is also hope for the rich. The Good News Gospel is God's truth revealing God's love.

But mailings only get you so far. Were people reading it? Was it touching hearts? What could we do next?

We decided to increase our presence on the streets. We preached from the corners in the spirit of Mr. Rogers's ministry, not in the confrontational tone that many people think of in the States.

We focused on goodness, light, and love. Yes, we preached sin, hell, and redemption, but we turned our eyes on the glory of the cross of Jesus Christ.

Our street preaching went well, but it didn't stop young Luis from dreaming. *How do we touch a city?* The question haunted me. There must be a way to do it. There must be an effective method to evangelize in the heart of a city, a region, or a country, exposing hundreds of thousands to the Good News.

Then came the book. Billy Graham was only twenty-nine, but he was impacting cities the way that I dreamed of doing. Graham, George Beverly Shea, Cliff Barrows, and Jerry Bevan—a central core of four—each worked as part of a larger unit. *That's it!* A vital truth clicked into place: an evangelist must have a team. No one could execute what was needed by themselves. And they didn't have to! God provided a diversity of giftings to empower the ministries of His people, including evangelism. The team didn't need to be big, but it had to be right. It had to be logistically strategic, suitably gifted, and spiritually focused.

I felt exhilarated. What if it *was* possible to reach entire cities with the Gospel? What if it *was* possible to leave a mark for Jesus on the heart of a nation or a culture? What if my dreams of ministry weren't just dreams? What if they were a *call?*

Billy's ministry used the radio. That got me thinking. My thinking quickly turned into doing, and through a whirlwind process I still don't understand (don't ask me how it was funded because I have absolutely no idea), I started preaching on the radio in Córdoba when I was still a young fellow.

With a man like Mr. Graham (he always insisted I call him Billy, but it never felt right), it's hard to know where to begin. He touched the whole world. He shaped history more deeply than most recognize. He also inspired me as a man and as an evangelist. He was my mentor. The facts about my relationship with Mr. Graham could be written on the back of a postcard:

- I saw him as an example and inspiration from the beginning of my ministry.
- I occasionally traveled with and interpreted for him.
- I learned the practical workings of his ministry directly from him and his team.
- He opened opportunities for and supported our team by his reputation and by giving us a little seed money.
- He remained my friend and an inspiration throughout his life.

It was quite simple really. But those five points do not even *begin* to capture what it was like to be close to Billy Graham. He was a giant of the faith, a lion with gentle eyes. I could fill books with the wisdom and inspiration I drew from him throughout our friendship.

While that midnight radio show in Argentina brought me his voice for the first time, I first met Billy in Córdoba before I came to the States. Although he was well known, it was still early in his career. Our meeting was so brief that I completely forgot about the encounter until *he* reminded me about it in a letter in 1991.

"I remember when I . . . first got acquainted with you in your hometown," he wrote. "What great expectations we had for you and your future, and the Lord has allowed you to more than fulfill them!"

It all came back as soon as he reminded me. I was about twenty-one and was the executive secretary of a small committee working to bring him to Argentina, which ended up preparing me for relating to the many volunteers who would do the same for me in coming decades. Our interactions were brief, but I helped show him around the city. Apparently it made more of an impression on him than on me! I was always amazed at his vote of confidence from the very beginning.

We did not stay in touch after that. I went on to hold my first campaign, plant my first church, and enroll at Multnomah. Not until Pat and I were married and completing our internship in Detroit did I have the opportunity to meet Mr. Graham again.

After Multnomah and our marriage, Pat and I joined a missionary agency named Overseas Crusades. If you recall, the director, Dick Hillis, had been a missionary in China. I told Dr. Hillis that my dream was to preach to crowds as a mass evangelist. I wanted to target the big cities. He told me they had room for my calling, and they accepted me as a team member based on my desire for evangelistic campaigns.

While we were wrapping up in Detroit and praying through our next steps, Dr. Hillis wrote to me:

> Billy Graham is having a campaign in Fresno, California. We at the mission want to send you and Pat to go learn the ropes of how to organize a united city-wide evangelistic campaign. You will be the assistant to the crusade director, Bill Brown, and Pat has work waiting for her at the office. Expenses covered, no salary. You'll stay in a farm down the road in Fresno.

Pat and I were thrilled. We had a chance to learn firsthand from the best.

We worked in Fresno for two and a half months, learning everything we possibly could. The director, Bill Brown, knowing that we were there to learn and not just for a short-term job, gave us carte-blanche permission to learn the full inner workings of how they did things.

"You want to evangelize like Billy?" he asked.

"Yeah," I said, "big city-wide campaigns are my goal."

"Okay," he said, "collect anything you want during your time here—materials, committee notes, examples of our print resources. Whatever you need, learn it here. Make your own crusade manual."

That generous permission set me free. I learned the logistics and tactics of a large-scale campaign from the inside.

A week before the event, Mr. Graham arrived. He held a breakfast for the team and our local supporters, about a hundred and fifty people total. We gathered in a hotel. Bill Brown intentionally seated Pat and me right next to Billy. The three of us started talking, and we immediately connected. I was his translator for the large Spanish-speaking population of the San Joaquin Valley. He had his secretary give me his sermons for every night of the campaign. "I want you to have all the time you need to think through the best way to translate them," he said. Getting my hands on his sermons sent a thrill through my preacher's heart!

As we talked throughout the meal, the conversation turned toward my heart to evangelize. He looked me right in the eyes and, with a weight that was both realistic and inspiring, said one of the most important pieces of advice I ever heard, one of the things that shaped my ministry. "Go to the big cities, Luis," he said. "Don't take too much time in the smaller towns. The big cities are like the tall mountains. When it rains on top of the mountain, the water flows downhill and waters every valley. The mountain is the city. When the Gospel rains there, it blesses the other places, but like water, it hardly ever flows uphill."

The event was beautiful. I stood on the side of the platform dedicated to those who spoke Spanish. I listened to Billy through a surplus WWII radio headset, pressing the receiver to my ear, then translating into a microphone for the Spanish-speaking crowd. How thrilling to be a small part of the conversions that week!

Luis's parents on their wedding day, 1934.

Infant Luis being held by his father in their hometown of Ingeniero Maschwitz, Argentina, 1935.

PREDICAMOS A CRISTO CRUCIFICADO

Luis's church community standing outside their small church building in Ingeniero Maschwitz, Argentina.

Luis (*front right*) with his father and three
of his sisters, Matilde, Martha, and Ketty.

Luis's family and church community. Edward Rogers (*back row, fifth from
the right*), Luis's father (*back row, second from the right*), Luis's mother (*front
row, third from the right*), and Luis's aunt (*front row, second from the right*).

Luis pictured with his mother, three of his sisters, and his little brother.

Luis's mother, Matilde Balfour de Palau.

Luis's school photo, 1955.

Luis and Pat cutting the cake on their wedding day, 1961. Immediately after their wedding they moved to Detroit, Michigan, to begin their missionary training.

Luis and Pat Palau, 1960.

Luis and Pat leading Sunday school during their missionary internship program in Detroit, Michigan.

Luis Palau, 1963.

Luis recording radio programs
in Acapulco, Mexico, 1964.

Luis preaching at his first major outdoor campaign in
the Plaza de Bolívar in Bogotá, Colombia, 1966.

Luis and Pat Palau, 1970.

Luis preaching in a church
in Cali, Colombia.

Luis preaching in Monterrey, Mexico, 1966.

Luis, Pat, and their young boys on the mission field.

Luis and Billy Graham walking the streets of Mexico City, 1972.

Pastor Ray Stedman from Palo Alto, California, 1960.

Luis interpreting for Billy Graham at a pastors'
gathering in Guatemala, 1976.

Luis with son Andrew playing the
piano. (We're pretty sure neither one
of them knows how to play.)

Luis Palau Evangelistic Team

Luis and Pat Palau
Keith, Kevin, Stephen and Andrew

Palau Family prayer card.

Luis speaking to students at Wheaton College.

Luis has been a regular guest on television programs throughout Latin America, the UK, and the US, speaking to the spiritual issues facing society and individuals.

Luis with his early team: (*from left to right*) John MacWilliams, Marcelino Ortiz, Luis, Bruce Woodman, and Jim Williams, 1977.

Luis sharing with youth in
Glasgow, Scotland, 1981.

Mission to London, Trafalgar Square Rally, 1983.

Luis and Billy Graham backstage during Mission to London, 1984.

As part of the massive, award-winning publicity campaign for Mission to London in 1984, posters were plastered across the city of London with slogans like "Bring Your Doubts" or "Take this Bus to QPR where Luis Palau will take you further."

Luis speaking with youth during a campaign in Bulgaria, 1991.

Luis preaching in Romania, 1990.

For many years Luis hosted live, call-in television programs called *Night Talk* in festival cities where he would answer tough spiritual questions and concerns from callers.

Luis, Pat, and their four sons, 2017.

Luis greeting kids during a CityServe clean
up date in Washington, DC, 2005.

Luis with Minister Zhao Qizheng, minister of information
for the People's Republic of China, 2005. They would go on to
become good friends and write a bestselling book together titled
A Friendly Dialogue Between an Atheist and a Christian.

Luis being interviewed by Dan Rather, 2008.

In 2008 Luis returned to his hometown to lead a major evangelistic campaign in Buenos Aires, Argentina. The effort brought together thousands of churches, tens of thousands of believers, and hundreds of thousands of individuals for the two-day festival in the heart of the city. It proved to be one of Luis's most historic and memorable campaigns.

Luis preaching in Times Square, New York. This event was part of a massive, three-month campaign to saturate New York City with the Gospel. Luis and the team partnered with more than 1,700 local churches to hold 115 evangelistic outreaches during the summer of 2015.

Luis and Pat with their sons, daughters-in-law, and grandkids.

Luis and his son Andrew preaching at a festival in Eugene, Oregon, 2018.

Luis with the entire Luis Palau Association staff from around the world, 2018. Luis has always said, "An evangelist without a team can do nothing."

When the campaign ended, Pat and I left for the mission field with the outline of a manual for future crusades lifted straight from the Graham playbook, ready to be adapted to our style and for our opportunities. Billy and his team had gone out of their way to train me and set me up for success. After Fresno, we began raising support for ministry in Colombia.

Fresno was only the beginning of learning from Mr. Graham, though. I kept an ear on his work—to the point that it began to drive Pat a little crazy. In the spring of 1962, we picked up some 33 rpm records from his crusade in Chicago earlier that year. I took six of them with us to Colombia when we moved there and played them endlessly, trying to get the hang of his rhythm, studying how he might have started with a joke or how he switched between the passage and his exposition. He had honed his preaching, every rise and fall of his voice, and I wanted to learn. Did I try to imitate him? No, I was a different man, a different preacher. But like a young painter looking over the shoulder of an established artist, I felt that I had so much to learn from his technique in preaching the Gospel to crowds. The repetition wore on Pat, poor woman! We could both recite those sermons in our sleep.

In Colombia, I hoped to start evangelizing to the masses like I'd discussed with Dr. Hillis. That was the reason we'd been sent to Fresno, after all. But time passed, and the opportunities weren't coming as fast as I wanted. My patience thinned and then evaporated in the Colombian heat.

I wrote a small stack of letters to the leadership. Many of them revealed my temper. They began to pile up, but Fred Renich's warning about my impatience and temper held me back from carrying the stack to the post office. I am so glad that I never mailed them. Though I was upset by the delay, Pat was right: I needed it. It was wise to hold me back. In those days, my passion and drive were greater than my ability to responsibly pull off those campaigns in a humble, effective way.

I don't pretend to know alternative histories, but it's entirely possible that if I had been given control, as I was tempted to demand, it could have been too much too soon. I tremble to think about it, but having seen other young evangelists crash and burn after a promising beginning, getting what I wanted then could have ended my ministry before it truly began.

So I waited. Things moved forward slowly. I traveled, preached, and began to assemble a team. Opportunities in Latin America came; souls were saved. We held a few small campaigns in Colombia, Ecuador, and Peru, but none were really in line with our dreams for a massive impact. I continually felt held back. Why wasn't I being let loose to do what I'd been called and trained to do?

Finally a remarkable opportunity came onto the horizon. Our first large mass evangelism campaign was to be held in the capital city of Bogotá. It was scheduled for December 1966, a time fraught with violence and simmering conflict. I hoped the campaign would be a key evangelical gathering, a symbolic march through the heart of the city, that peaceably shouted, *We are here!* to the city and the nation. It would be attended by thousands and would surely attract the attention of thousands more.

Imagine my surprise when I got a letter from Billy's team. They invited me to Berlin that October for a worldwide congress on evangelism. The invitation challenged us to "Let the whole world hear the voice of God," and my heart burned for just that.

I flew from Colombia to Germany by myself, with only fifty dollars in my pocket. Berlin still bore the scars of the war. It was a remarkable backdrop for a conversation about carrying the message of Christ's peace to all peoples.

I was just one of the attendees, but I mingled and met people I knew from the radio or the pages of *Christianity Today*, the American magazine Billy founded. In those days, *Christianity Today* was an example of everything that I hoped for Latin America, presenting evangelical faith as intelligent and secure in its beliefs, neither cowering in fear or falling prey to the temptation to advance its interests through dirty politics or other underhanded means.

I only briefly connected with Billy at the opening reception, but his invitation helped give me confidence that the ministry I felt called to was the right path to follow.

I remember walking the bitterly cold and snowy streets of Berlin with a friend from the conference, eating Wiener schnitzel and just talking. My eyes had been opened to new possibilities by being at the congress. I had received the encouragement my impatient heart needed. The congress had expanded my understanding of how God was working to spread the Good News. This world *could* be impacted by everyday people. A man like me *could* make a difference.

After all, Billy Graham had done it, right? It seemed like the whole world was waiting for our message.

Mr. Graham's humility was seen by many. When we walked into a room and there was someone he hadn't met, he would simply walk up and extend his hand, saying without a hint of irony, "Hi, I'm Billy Graham." Not affected, not fake, no Southern-cutesy. He was really *meeting* them.

After televangelist Jim Bakker had his meteoric fall from grace and went to prison for fraud, I hear that he was assigned toilet-cleaning duty on Christmas morning. While in the thick of the job, a voice came across the intercom: "Jim Bakker, visitor!"

It was Billy Graham. Jim, fresh out of toilet duty, went to see his visitor and says simply that Billy threw his arms around Jim and said, "Jim, I love you." Billy had every reason to think that visit was beneath him. Yet he went straight to the source of the mess and embraced it, just like Jesus. Billy genuinely loved people, and he did not judge them. I believe that's what made him one of the most remarkable witnesses for the Good News in history. Was he flawed? Yes, of course, as we all are. Do I fall down and worship him as some kind of hero? Not in the least.

But he was and remains a true inspiration.

Everything Billy taught me, by word and deed, was formative. But it was nothing new. It was the same advice that mentors in the faith have been giving their disciples since the beginning of Christianity: be humble. That's all. Every Christian should embrace humility, and every pastor should ground their ministry in it. But do we live it? Are we strong enough to give up our pride?

We were in Germany once at a German congress on evangelism. While we were in Billy's hotel room, a young German Lutheran evangelist came in to speak to Billy after Billy's assistant, T. W. Wilson, let the young man through.

The young man came in and practically kissed Billy's hand. "What did you want to talk about?" Billy asked after their greetings.

"I was converted when you came to Germany years ago," he said, "and I was called to be an evangelist. I went to seminary, have a team—seventeen of us—and have money. But I have no invitations to preach. Nobody invites me. Could you give me some suggestions?"

Billy looked utterly at a loss—never in his ministry had he lacked speaking invitations. He looked at his team members to help him think of something. They talked about a few possibilities, and as they were concluding, the young preacher asked, "Mr. Graham, would you bless me?"

"Of course. Let's pray," Billy said, and led us to our knees. He began to pray for this fellow he'd never met before.

I don't know what I was expecting, but whatever I expected was a lot shorter than what happened. Billy prayed and *prayed*. He prayed up a storm for the young man. This was not some token prayer of blessing to send the young buck off. He was sincere. "Lord, bless this young man. Open doors for him. Give him chances to win souls, Father . . ."

While we were praying, Billy's voice became muffled. I opened my eyes, curious. Billy Graham was flat on his face with his arms spread out. His nose and mouth were pressed into the hotel room carpet. And the prayer just kept coming.

I was so moved. He was the most famous evangelist in the world—indeed, one of the best-known Christians in history. His preaching influence? Incalculable. Presidents waited for his phone call. Yet here he was in a wholly unnecessary (or so I thought!) posture of complete humility. Surely God could have heard him just as well from his knees, right? Or a chair at least?

When the prayers were finished, we all rose to our feet—Billy rising from lower than the rest. The young man thanked Billy, and Billy's assistant escorted him out. Then I made some comment to Billy. I don't even remember what I said. I do remember his response: "Look, Luis, when it says in 1 Peter 5, 'Humble yourselves therefore under the mighty hand of God, that he may exalt you in due time' . . . Luis, we have to practice that."

I never learned the young man's name. I don't know if he ever got his chance to preach. But I will never forget the sound of Billy Graham's voice muffled by the carpet of a German hotel. That must be what humility sounds like.

This was illustrated further by a colorful experience that still makes me chuckle. Pat and I were flying into Los Angeles, California, where we were scheduled for a meeting with Mr. Graham at a local hotel. We landed at LAX and began looking around for someone from the Graham team. Then a mysterious figure caught our attention. He was tall, dressed like a dime-store spy, complete with dark glasses, a floppy Elmer Fudd style hat, and—you can't make this stuff up—*a false nose*. Of course it was Billy Graham. For some reason, he had decided to drive us back to the hotel himself. Pat pointed out that his disguise attracted more attention to himself, and we all had a good laugh. His incredible, simple humility, his willingness to put on a disguise to welcome us—I will never forget it. It was funny, but more than anything it was kind.

Who is your example of humility? Who has not only *told* you but *shown* you what it means to humble yourself before God? Those examples are invaluable.

The most intelligent theologian, the most eloquent expositor, the most careful scholar—they cannot hold a candle to a Christian who is willing to get on their face under the mighty hand of God. No teaching can replace it, no preaching can prompt it, and no research can deepen it. Only a genuine, inner conviction—a desperation for becoming nothing before God—can carry that kind of spiritual power. How rich, how deep, how mysterious is the work of God, who meets us upon the floor, who listens as we pray into carpets. Praise Him!

Evangelists are not easily satisfied. We tend to feel the burden of every empty seat in the crowd. It can be easy, especially when you're young, to lose perspective. It was encouraging to find out that Billy struggled with this too. "Even when you think the stadium will be full, it may not be," he once told me. "So change your expectations. I've learned to hope for whatever room I'm preaching in—church or stadium—to be half full. Anything more than that? I'm exhilarated."

Evangelism leaves no place for braggadocio. Ministry is *never* about us. How quickly our humility can simply become a showpiece virtue.

This is why Billy Graham's example did more for my heart than nearly any other. Seeing up close the authenticity and integrity of his ministry inspired me to do the simple things that fuel a person's inner life. It inspired me to continually heed Ray's call to crucify my ego. It made me feel both completely seen and valued by God, yet it also showed God's willingness to use *anyone* willing to empty themselves in humility. The moment this hotshot from Argentina started to feel like an indispensable part of God's plan, I'd see in my mind's eye the moment that these lips would turn to clay, and I would seek anew the joyous weight of God's mighty hand as I'd been shown it by my teacher, encourager, mentor, friend, and heartfelt example, Billy Graham.

Later in life, Billy's letters became shorter and shorter, eventually taking the form of apologies—usually for not being able to communicate effectively on a call that we'd had. His handwriting became shakier and shakier as Parkinson's slowly took its due from him, until finally they simply stopped, replaced by kind notes from his longtime secretary. The great man's journey continued into the dark suffering of his long-lasting illness. It was on the day that he died, February 21, 2018, that I fully committed to writing this book.

Honestly, being called the Billy Graham of Latin America was a little embarrassing at the beginning. After all, *Billy Graham* was the Billy Graham of Latin America! But I am still honored, though I've never called myself that. I see my unworthiness of that title.

Pride is a unique vice, because it can be so disconnected from any real thing. The most prideful people are often those with the least right to be. It is all in their mind and in their heart. A prideful person's self-image is unmoored from their abilities, accomplishments, or achievements.

But praise God, humility can be a virtue of the same kind of disconnection! Just as one can be prideful with not a single reason to support it, so can one be genuinely humble when you have every reason in the world, in earthly terms, to puff yourself up.

Can you think of a preacher with more cause for pride than Billy Graham? The man was a confidant of presidents, a friend to world leaders. He led more people to Jesus than live in some countries! His integrity was unquestioned; his faithfulness to the Gospel, remarkable. When you boil down the words of all his critics, the worst they can say of him—other than to mention his few very poorly chosen political and racial comments, which he deeply regretted—is that he was too willing to work for unity in the church and love in the world. That is a legacy that could have made a veritable monster of pride out of that dairy farmer's boy from North Carolina.

But did it? No. Never did I know him to gloat, puff himself up, indulge in smugness, or pat himself on the back, even in our private conversations. He viewed his accomplishments with honesty and immediately credited his successes to God and the hard work of many others. His simplicity of spirit was profound.

Ego has always dogged me. A real temptation to pride runs to my core. I'm sure that temptation was there for Billy—why else would he have advised me to resist pride unless the temptation was real? If I did not have his example towering above me, I could have gradually slipped into a personal life defined by pride. I could have hidden it well, but it would have soured everything I did. Praise God, I think that I genuinely avoided pride. Not perfectly, but consistently.

How about you, reader? Where is your heart? Is it giving in to the profound temptation of pride? Or is it humbling itself beneath the mighty hand responsible for all our victories? Whether we are lowly or exalted, God's hands can touch our lips—even if they are of clay—and free them to speak His Good News.

We all can make a difference for the world's good and God's glory. If—and that is an enormous "if"—we are willing to become nothing so that God can become everything in us.

CHAPTER 8

So Much Better Than Alone

The Luis Palau Association Team

> Two are better than one, because they have a
> good return for their labor.
>
> ECCLESIASTES 4:9

Mass evangelism tends to be accompanied by the temptation to corrupt the calling. Crowds gather. People listen—a *lot* of people. It is a short hop from there to begin thinking of yourself as a celebrity, as a ministry movie star. Your goal of introducing people to Jesus can be easily taken over by that nagging temptation to make this about *you*.

This temptation makes having a team so important. If you are a narcissistic, insecure leader, you will probably build a team that reflects and reinforces your behavior. Instead, it is vital to have strong supporters of the mission who are not merely tools of personal loyalty.

I have recently realized that I spent my entire life going full speed ahead, with the accelerator to the floor. Next thing, next thing, next thing. There have been wonderful advantages to the fast pace. It is part of the reason we have been able to do so much. But I have also let the past simply flow away from me for much of my life. *Somebody else better record and remember this*, I'd think. *I don't have time to waste on it.* But I see now that it is not a waste. Our story is God's story as much as ours.

Though I've always had an independent streak, I praise God that I never gave in to the temptation to go it alone. Not that the temptation was strong, mind you. I'm too much of a one-trick pony to have gotten far without help! Still, I thank God that I didn't give in to that temptation. From my first days of street preaching to today, as I watch a remarkably talented and well-honed team prepare to continue the ministry without me, I have been unbelievably blessed to be part of a team much larger, much wiser, much stronger, and *infinitely* more effective than I ever could have been solo. "If you want to go fast, go alone," says one African proverb, "but if you want to go far, go together."

That "together" has included the whole body of Christ (more on that in a couple chapters) and even those outside the faith. It includes everyone from "random" strangers to heads of state, from one-time volunteers to those who spent their entire careers on our team. How I wish I could honor each of those men and women by name!

God tells some of His best stories in a whisper. You have to pay careful attention to catch them. You could walk right past some of the most incredible miracles without batting an eye.

Of all the campaigns that we've done across the world, a few stand out as clearly miraculous. Leningrad (now St. Petersburg) in 1989 is one. What unbelievable open doors were shown us by the Soviet Union, a country most considered "closed"! Hong Kong in 1987 was another—the hush of the stadium as I asked everyone to turn their eyes upward to the stars and think about who made them, and seeing thousands flood the field that night in commitment to Jesus. Guatemala City in 1982 was one of our largest gatherings ever, with hundreds of thousands of people. New York City in 2015—we'll save that story for later. I could go on and on.

Of all the quiet miracles and all the special campaigns, one stands out as the most memorable of my career: the United Kingdom, in the campaign leading up to (and including) Mission to London in 1983–1984.

This campaign required great stamina and creativity from our team. It required profound dependence upon the spiritual leading, invitation, and provision of God through the Welsh, the Scots, and the English. It is the story of quiet and unknown people.

The story really begins at Eurofest in 1975, a youth conference that Billy Graham's team put together. I was one of the speakers, and the Spirit of God touched the event in an *amazing* way. About ten thousand young people came from all over Europe and the Middle East. Remarkable things happened, including reconciliation between former Israeli and Egyptian soldiers, still fresh with memories from the Six-Day War. Both sides embraced, hugging and kissing, asking for forgiveness.

I was a last-minute addition to the schedule because the original speaker had fallen ill. I spoke from the story of Joseph, and the response was something special. When I invited those who needed prayer or counseling to come forward, thousands stood—about seven thousand I later heard. It was overwhelming. My teammate Jim Williams, a veteran of our Latin American crusades, sprang into action, quickly organizing a way for pastors and missionaries attending the conference to join and talk with those requesting support, prayer, or biblical counseling. What a moment, seeing these young people surging forward to renew their commitment to holy living and a faith whose popularity was at the lowest ebb in recent memory on their continent. God was moving.

At the end of the conference, a man approached me. "Would you ever bring a campaign to Wales?" he asked. "I'm from Cardiff."

"I'd love to," I replied. "Invite me!"

"I'm inviting you right now," he said. As we talked, my gut said, *This fellow's dreaming. He's not going to be able to pull the backing together for a campaign.*

"As soon as you have a gang of people, invite me," I said as we finished talking. "I don't care how big or small it is. I just want to preach in the UK."

Well, he proved my gut wrong. Soon enough, he wrote. "We're ready," he said. He had a group of churches, a venue, a plan for getting people there. He'd even booked Cliff Richards—a singer as big in the UK as Elvis Presley was in the States, who at Eurofest had shared a beautiful testimony of faith in the resurrected Lord Jesus.

We held the campaign at the castle in Cardiff in 1977. It was a symbolic setting for the Welsh. That simple campaign, prompted by a single invitation from one man, opened surprising doors. After Cardiff, a farmer from Aberdeen, Scotland, approached me. He looked like you'd expect, smiling, a bit weather-beaten, like he came from a land of green grass, gray skies, and white sheep. He grew rye for making bread. He had big hands and a slow way of talking. "Would you consider, Mr. Palau," he said with a thick Scottish accent, "coming to Aberdeen?"

"I'd love to," I said, thinking, *Anything in Britain—I'll take it!*

He was just an elder at a little church, but somehow he managed to get us a soccer stadium. He booked Pittodrie Stadium, to be precise, which seats over 22,000. So I found myself at the North Sea, where the wind off the water cuts straight to your bones—even in summer. "Everyone loves Scotland from a distance," I remember someone joking. The bitter wind was a chilly welcome to one of the countries of my ancestors. But the people were warm, and the farmer's invitation turned into a glorious campaign.

Other towns and villages opened from there, as we spent months crisscrossing Scotland and then began a wonderful time of holding tent meetings throughout England. What a remarkable reversal of my boyhood! Mr. Rogers had preached in tents in my country. Now I was preaching in tents in his! And the months stretched on. All told, I estimate that we preached in about one hundred towns and villages in England plus over thirty in Scotland. We spent two weeks of tent preaching in and around Motherwell and five weeks in Glasgow preaching in Kelvin Hall. We held meetings seven days a week in Glasgow and saw many saved. By the end, I felt that I had seen more of beautiful Britain than most Brits get to see!

Along the way, miracles of salvation were happening. I am always impressed by spiritual miracles. I love to see people come into a real and vibrant faith when there is no explanation for their decision other than the Holy Spirit. Yet victory implies battles. No progress can be made without a fight. Our enemy constantly seeks to disrupt unity, to disturb us, and to set us at odds with one another. So one of the great victories of our time in the UK was the sustained unity that it brought to people from many different denominations, regions, ethnicities, and ways of thinking—urban and rural; Scots, Welsh, Irish, and English; mainline and evangelical. How powerful it was to see each person fighting their own battles but joining the cause that had brought us all together. By God's grace, what could have been a fractured, abrasive time was united by a common good.

The British are slow to commit spiritually, but when they

do, they mean it. That's why the miraculous numbers of people and tent meetings during that time mean so much to me. On the closing night of two weeks in Motherwell, the chairman, who introduced me every night when I gave the final invitation, stood up. He came forward with his wife and two children, turned to the crowd, and said, "We receive Jesus Christ." He was chairing the outreach but wasn't assured of his own relationship to Jesus. He left that tent with full confidence in his salvation. He had found assurance of eternal life, which his family had never had until that campaign.

Our team members regularly report meeting British people across the globe who made a significant decision for Jesus because of our time in the UK: missionaries, teachers, activists, pastors, business leaders, international students, and more. The trip not only helped lead to conversions, but God gave our time in the UK a special blessing that energized people to serve the kingdom. When Jay Fordice, the creative director of Luis Palau Association (LPA), went back to Scotland in 2008, he met so many pastors and people in ministry who all look back to Glasgow as a key moment in their story. The legacy of these events reaches around the world. It's beautiful. It's all because of God.

And the work and preaching progressed. Glasgow led to Leeds, and Leeds to London.

My plan had long been that if the Lord brought someone who invited us to London, we would accept immediately. We spread the word fast and told everyone we could, so we could get there before someone stepped in and pushed us out. So we formed a group, unifying our connections. It was led in part by Scots like the young businessman George Russell. We called it Mission to London.

I had long had my sights on London because of its unique potential for global impact. Only a few other metropolises in the world have similar influence. Billy had told me that the big cities were like tall mountains. If so, then London was a towering peak.

Its strategic influence would be incalculable. So was its spiritual neediness, and so were the challenges.

Imagine for a moment that you were tasked with pulling off an event with a hundred thousand people in the heart of one of the world's great cities. Where would you start? Where would you find the money? How would you mobilize churches, approach the city government, handle security, and spread the word? Just think about the monumental logistical challenges.

Our plan had two stages over a two-year period. First, we would hold small campaigns in ten key areas of the city to build momentum and support. The second phase would last six weeks and be held in a prime location: The Queen's Park Rangers Football Stadium. The stadium was prestigious and the *perfect* size: not so small that we'd need to turn people away yet not so large that it would be in danger of feeling empty with anything short of a monumental turnout.

As always, local churches led the way. We were leery, especially with the British, to impose anything from outside. We served, supported, and walked with them, but the British church carried leadership and logistics. It went beautifully. "Bring Your Doubts" read posters throughout the city in a major ad campaign. We got significant media coverage. Headlines said things like "Hard Task Ahead for Luis Palau" and "Born Again, The Ballyhoo Battle for Britain."

The first phase, in 1983, went well. I did get the flu, but a few other preachers filled in for me. This was one of only a couple times in my entire life that someone else had to fill in for me. The events in phase one were mostly held in tents and were great successes. As we drew nearer to the second phase, a lot of people began to second-guess our plan. The expense alone would be enormous. The local committee working to bring us there were, frankly, daunted. It was obvious that the endeavor would be impossible, short of unity and provision that needed to be a flat-out miracle.

So the committee sent me to talk with Sir Morris Laing.

Sir Morris was the son of a well-known Christian philanthropist. His father had first come into his own as a developer between the wars, and his business grew greatly during the rebuilding of England after the destruction of World War II.

My objective was to represent the local committee and gain his support—his voice nearly as much as his "chequebook."

"Who is Sir Morris?" I asked.

"Go visit him," they replied.

A friend arranged for my private appointment at 11:30 a.m. one morning. I remember it exactly. To be honest, after all the buildup, I went into the meeting a bit awed. After all, I was about to meet one of the wealthiest men in Europe.

I walked in punctually. He greeted me with surprising curtness. "'Morning," he said, in a bit of a sharp British way. "Tea?"

"Yes, please," I said, even less at ease.

"Sugar?"

"Yes."

"Milk?"

"Yes, please."

He poured for the two of us, and we sat. I sipped gingerly, breathing the warm steam. "I have fifteen minutes for you," he said. "I must go to the city to meet with the head of Royal Dutch Shell and another business partner. So . . ." He sipped his tea politely, looking me hard in the eye. "What do you want from me?"

Wow! Walk into a stranger's office to a greeting like that? But he was not being unkind, just sternly direct, as a man in his position must be.

"Well, sir," I began, "I don't want anything from you. But the executive committee for our evangelistic London campaign told me that they are under extreme financial pressure, and that God has given you contacts and resources that may be able to help us."

"Yes," he replied. "some foundations and trusts."

"I wouldn't know. I'm not really familiar with how things work here in Britain," I said. "But they told me that you have a heart for the city and the nation."

"I know what they want," he said. He got up, went to his check-book with a pen, and came back. With a check for 100,000 pounds.

"Will this do?" he asked. That is a large sum today. But then it seemed astronomical.

"I think it will encourage the committee," I said with a chuckle.

"Good," he said. "I've been asking around carefully about you. I don't want to get involved in anything that might give my business a bad name. But you seem honorable. There is another check for that same amount if you come up short at the end. Please tell no one because I do not like to give alone. Let's get others involved."

At a quarter till, he said a polite goodbye and left for his other appointment after fifteen minutes on the nose. I walked out of there beaming. I walked to lunch with the committee. When I pulled the check out of my pocket, they all gasped. Then the committee chairman pulled an envelope out of his jacket. "This is of the Lord," the chairman said. "I have a letter of resignation in my pocket. If he had not given this, I couldn't have carried on—I wouldn't have had the courage."

Sir Morris joining our efforts threw open the doors to the highest levels of British society and life. At the invitation of several key supporters, I began to hold coffee hours all over greater London. We even partnered on a prayer breakfast event for parliamentarians at the Speaker's house, which is still an annual event more than thirty years later. In those days, which were fresh after the Falkland War between the UK and Argentina, it was nearly unthinkable for an Argentine to be doing this and for the British to respond so favorably. But it happened.

All the press got people talking. Papers, magazines, TV, and radio contributed to the swell of interest. Even the newspapers were featuring cartoons about the mission. Meanwhile, we held dozens of events touching every level of British society—tea always featuring prominently—to further prepare for the stadium preaching.

My message, especially at high-society women's events, was always the same: the story of the Samaritan woman. I would read the story, we would have special music, and then, for some incomprehensible reason, we had a *mime* who would perform. I dislike mimes intensely by nature. I think they're creepy. But this fellow nearly convinced me of the value of a mime. He really acted out his message effectively. I had a different message prepared titled "Five Kinds of Women," but my wife, always insightful, asked, "Who are you to talk about women?" I had to admit she had a good point.

Lady Susie Sainsbury, a highly respected socialite whose husband is now a member of the House of Lords, had become a friend. She suggested the story of the Samaritan woman at the well. "Are you sure?" I asked. "These are high-society ladies." We'd be talking about a woman with a reputation who'd had five husbands and was living with a sixth man. At one event, where two hundred of the wealthiest women in Britain were gathered at the Hurlingham Club, Suzy smiled wryly. "See that woman in blue over there?" She pointed at an elegant figure across the room. "We were at university together, and *let me tell you* . . ."

"Okay, okay, okay, I get it," I said hastily.

These were people like everyone else. For all their veneer, they had the same sins, spiritual hungers and thirsts, and need for the Good News of Jesus. I spoke, and a good number came to the Lord. As a result, they started two regular Bible studies among these women of high standing. Much of the world doesn't understand the British caste system, but this was a miracle—a social miracle but a miracle nonetheless. What other name can you give it when someone goes against the taboos and cultural etiquette for the sake of Jesus?

It takes courage for high-society people to openly express their Christian convictions. Those circles of high education, finance, title, and influence often frown on those who make a point of their faith beyond a weekly Sunday social event. And to go so far as to even *hint* that one ought to believe in Jesus is a big deal! People of high social standing put their reputation on the line with a decision like that. They could lose a lot of friends if people started whispering, "Do you know who's become a fundamentalist?"

In the first stage of the Mission, about 200,000 Londoners attended our events. Of those, 8,000 made public commitments to follow Jesus. I preached "the same old thing," as C. S. Lewis wryly called it, the Good News. In that second phase of ministry in London, over 20,000 people made public commitments to Jesus—I am not sure the total number of people who came, but it was immense. Who knows how many in the privacy of their own hearts met God?

As always, I preached about the need for an encounter with the living Christ, the centrality of the Bible, and the incredible goodness of God's grace. I spoke of God moving in Britain, drawing people into His family and His *friendship*, not merely His worship, not solely His lordship. I preached about the kind and loving Fatherhood of God and about His everlasting commitment of love.

Matt Redman, the now well-known worship musician, was converted there as a young boy, as were many future pastors, theologians, and missionaries. The impact was astounding, both in the short and long term. Billy Graham was right. The cities are mountains. Climbing this one had been hard but worth it.

There are many highlights from our team's ministry, but Mission to London is right there at the top. Fifteen weeks! To me, that's not just a campaign; it's a *campaign*. It's not like a mosquito biting an elephant; it is like someone starting to really *eat* the elephant.

Our success started in those little steps, one after the other—a fellow in Cardiff, a farmer in Aberdeen, and countless others whose full stories I don't have time to tell, like the moneylender in Ayrshire and the bookstore owner in Motherwell. Each story is another glorious step, all culminating in our being welcomed to London by Princess Alexandra—the queen's first cousin and personal friend.

One day when I was a young man in Argentina, I stood on a street corner in the little town where we ended up planting our first church. I was standing among a handful people, and in a flash of realization, I thought, *This is what the apostle Paul felt*, and not just Paul but *every* itinerant evangelist from the beginning of Christianity.

I stood there in a new town, surrounded by people I had never met. Possibly for the first time, they had been clearly presented with the Good News. A few people listened and were converted. Where before there had been no light, a little spark. *This is sacred business*, I thought. *I'm not just some nobody shouting John 3:16. I am a priest of God.* I knew that this whole business was too important, too dangerous, and too special to be attempted alone.

The Christian model of ministry is a team. Christ picked the twelve disciples. He sent the seventy-two out in pairs. Paul had seven with him in Acts 20. They all worked together. Paul was seldom alone. Sometimes Paul went with only one other person, everyone else having been sent out on one mission or another, but he still had help, backup, encouragement. No one has all the gifts of the body of Christ. We need each other desperately.

Pat brought a whole new dimension to what "team" meant. By

the time we got to Mexico in 1968, after our Bogotá festival in 1966 and after it was obvious that we were headed for extensive international ministry, we had a team of four men that proved to be the beginning of something special. Pat and I were the cofounders of this growing team.

One of my greatest mistakes is that I didn't give Pat the credit she deserved—not only as a spouse but as a teammate in every way. I honored her, of course, but I see now that it could have been dismissed as the lip service that many male preachers or teachers give to their wives. I should have done it officially and constantly until people saw the extent of her contribution. She was so much more than the smiling spouse. She did far more than people would ever guess, at every level of our ministry. Her commitment was total.

Our teammates had to have what Pat and I called "the missionary spirit"; that is, they had to be willing to live and work like we did—expecting nothing, demanding nothing, simply doing what we did because we were called. Let's face it, you don't get into evangelism because you're looking for a nice house and retirement account. Maybe that will come one day if the Lord chooses to provide. If that was what we wanted, we would have chosen a different path in life. Maybe comforts or security will come. But maybe they won't. Be ready for *won't*.

With that said, "staff" and "team" are different. Staff come and go more freely. It's important for them to be "in," but they are not here from a profound sense of calling. For team members, however, their investment is high, personal, and often lifelong. I think of team members like Doug Steward, who joined when he was a single student at Multnomah. He has a married son now. Jim Williams, David Jones, Ruben Proietti, John Ogle, Carlos Barbieri, Colin James, Anne Scofield, Edmundo Gastaldi, Scott Kraske, Levi Park—I could go on and on. So many men and women have given their careers to our mission.

This team is here because they want millions to hear. They want nations to be blessed and the church to be made stronger. They give and give for Christ's vision, which is larger than any of us. That vision doesn't change. Nor does their passion change, especially for those of our human family who are lost. This team simply wants to be a part of Christ's beautiful process of bringing what has been dead into new life, of finding what has been lost. Our whole team, from the board of directors to the temporary staff at far-flung festivals, shares this passion.

Ultimately, I have always seen myself as a member of the team. Many people, Ray Stedman included, critiqued my choice to use my name as part of the organization. But I couldn't escape this foundational truth: people listen to *people*. If you say to them, "Come hear a Gospel presentation on the assurance of eternal life," they'll reply, "You're nuts." If you say, "Come listen to this fellow from Argentina, Luis Palau," they'll say, "When is he speaking?" That's not self-promotion; it's human nature.

Obviously, our calling was to mass evangelistic ministry. But we had specific outcomes in mind from the very beginning that shaped how we implemented that calling.

One of our dreams was to revive God's people. We tried to teach them the principles of victorious Christian living, of overcoming, of living consistently with God's will for their own good and the good of their neighborhood and nation.

Church planting was always in the forefront. The missionaries who led us to Jesus had a very clear progression—get saved, get baptized, start a church. We wanted to encode those values into the LPA ministry from the beginning. We were not a replacement for the local church. We were here to empower and support it. And, of course, we're part of the church ourselves!

Passion for the local church was an essential quality for our team members. We would not bring on people who spoke disdainfully of Christ's body, as if they were coming to us to do the "real" work that local churches didn't have the brains or bravery to undertake. Such immaturity had no place at an LPA desk. We were servants of Christ, of the church, and of the lost whom Jesus would go to any lengths to bring to Himself. We existed for the benefit of others.

We used to keep a record of how many churches we'd been instrumental in starting. We stopped counting after about five thousand—because we'd simply become too busy. We didn't call ourselves a church planting ministry because that would have confused people. Having too many public objectives doesn't help a ministry. But the goal of planting churches was foundational, shared, and discussed by the whole team. In the two years after our historic campaign in Romania, we heard of hundreds of new church plants (through a Lausanne Movement report), many of them house churches, as a direct result of our team's work. That's to the glory of God alone. But I'll tell you, it is a very fulfilling feeling. This was the dream God gave me, *and God was fulfilling it!*

We didn't just sow the seed or convert individuals. Churches were planted by the thousands. To God be the glory.

I knew that having good crowds helps give you a hearing. People say that there isn't anything magic about numbers, and they're right. Except when they're not. Jesus doesn't need crowds to work, and many of His most incredible miracles and teachings happened quietly. But to touch the public life of a nation with the Good News, you need large numbers of people to open doors to the media and beyond. Crowds give you a hearing. Ordinary people listen to you in a new way. Big meetings open bigger doors.

Another vital requirement for a team member is genuine love for all people. You must steel yourself to love people who insult you. That whole "pray for those who curse you" thing isn't easy. Well, it is easy to quote Jesus on that one but mighty hard to practice it.

Then there's faith. You need faith to stay the course. Burnout is real. Billy Graham used to observe that most evangelists burn out after ten years. I suspect that's true for anyone following a demanding calling. The reasons are many, but one of them, quite frankly, is that over time people are tempted to talk more than they believe. Overtalking is a danger—going over the top, little by little, until people have a public image of you as a "Christian superstar" that doesn't match who you are inside. It is only a matter of time before such a ministry collapses on itself. After all, what else can it do? It's become bigger on the outside than the supporting faith within. What will hold it up? It's hollow.

Then there is choosing humility, which is easier said than done. We must crucify the flesh. There we find Christ's humility.

The best way that I know to stay humble is simply not to dwell on yourself. Have you had a wonderful victory? Praise the Lord for it and celebrate. Then allow it to fade into the past as surely as if it had been a disappointment. Look forward to Christ. If you concentrate on the past, you tend to inflate your own role, and if you are not careful, you may begin to feel that you deserve some of the credit and glory. Don't gloat. At best we are weak servants. Don't spend too much time trying on the Master's hat and looking in the mirror.

In the end, the key is this: a team member spends time with God. The rest—the love, the vision, the faith, the humility—comes from one's closeness to Jesus. After we spend time in God's presence, we glow. Others notice it. You yourself can *feel* it. Nothing else can replace time in God's presence. In His light, all darkness flees, for it knows it cannot overcome Him.

Our team is part of what gained us acceptance all over the world. Our team members walked with humility, servant attitudes, and the understanding that we existed to bless the church. That attitude becomes part of your reputation. Their excellence enhanced my reputation, the reputation of our ministry, and the reputation of Jesus too.

People think more highly of me than they should, but that is because of the team! People take the team's excellent work and ascribe it to me. Their work is the only part of me that some people see. They think they know me. But they really know the team members.

Over the decades I have drummed certain phrases into our team. One of the key ones is simply: *Proclaim!* Not just preach, *proclaim.* It has all the force and freshness of an authoritative announcement of Good News, which is precisely what the Gospel is.

As the team grew, there were challenges I'm afraid that I myself was one of the key challenges. In the first stages of our ministry, we'd bring in a talented, driven partner and send him or her to start preparing a city, but we would give them almost no direction. Then, to add insult to injury, I'd get upset when they didn't do exactly what I had in mind. It was really my responsibility to lead according to their needs, not only mine. Come on, Luis!

I often simply assumed too much. I would have been a better leader to have been more hands-on. My own weaknesses held the team back in certain ways. But it helped when I was challenged, kindly, by one of the team members I'd put into a difficult position this way. "Why don't you just write down what you want us to do?" he said, exasperated. "Instead, you're dumping us into cities, and we don't know what you really want. We know you want to get a crowd. Okay. *How?*" That feedback made a huge difference and led me to consider how my failure to clearly communicate expectations was a leadership problem that I had to overcome.

God gives vision to certain people as part of a call to leadership. He also calls many to support those leaders pursuing their divinely given calling. Both callings are vital. My philosophy of leadership largely came from the New Testament examples in Acts and the Epistles, especially 1 and 2 Timothy and Titus. I always encourage young leaders to study those letters word for word.

True leaders are a few steps ahead in terms of vision. A leader promotes and pushes that vision, and people respond. *Yes! He's saying exactly what I want to hear somebody say. I can follow this person!*

An evangelist tends to have a leading spirit. Evangelism demands strategy, drive, anointing, and the kind of love for people and trust in God that can't be faked or replaced. If God ordered it, it can be done. Therefore, let's do it! That's the kind of simple faith evangelistic ministry requires. Billy Graham loved the phrase, "O earth, earth, earth, hear the voice of the Lord!" The idea of calling nations to be awake in Christ through proclamation is so powerful.

A light, inspiring touch brings this kind of leadership. Many politicians, and sometimes even church people, think that powerful leaders have to impose their will like a dictator. Nothing could be further from the truth. All dictatorship does is set you up for a revolution (just read up on Latin American history for a crash course on *that* principle). You can't win that way; you're just kicking people around.

Inspiring people's vision is key when you are leading them into the work of winning others to Jesus. But that vision will quickly grow stale if it is not maintained. To keep the team growing and sharp, there needs to be a sense of stamina and a sense of identity that is wholly *for* the mission but also *bigger* than the mission. Our vision was kept alive by our consistent gathering and praying, talking and joking, eating and celebrating. We worked alongside one another, but we also genuinely cared for one another and our families. That connection was invaluable. After all, our lives were in one another's hands—literally. Our safety, mission, and reputation depended upon each other's trust, skill, and prayer.

Our team also includes supporters, who have given sacrificially and prayed with power. I marvel when I think that we have people who have supported us for fifty-five years. It is inspiring to think about everyone's faithfulness to our shared vision.

When you start to consider your life, and your mind begins to go back, you realize just how much the Lord was there. He was ahead of you the whole time, waiting patiently, speaking gently, inviting you. He was in distant countries long before we were. He was in Colombia, Scotland, England, China, Eastern Europe, and everywhere else I went. There were many times that it felt like a whole campaign was about to fall apart. There are many forces at work when you are leading a united campaign in a big city, and some problems can quickly become serious: interdenominational dynamics, political problems, enemies who hate the very essence of what you stand for. We got death threats, bomb threats, and more, though we never publicized them. These things all went on behind the scenes. And the team carried them as we prayed hard and worked to protect one another.

You're not putting on a show. You're not pretending. Spiritual warfare is real. Team members engage in the prayer and resistance of spiritual warfare throughout every phase of an evangelism campaign even as they sit beside the platform or smile and shake hands with volunteers.

Our team struggled in special ways together. But we also laughed in special ways together. As you see the drama behind the scenes, you see the humor too.

This team, through the grace and power of the Holy Spirit, has had global reach. It is remarkable what has been done. The sheer logistics of pulling off major events in distant nations, where security may be challenging, politics may be complicated, and solid details are elusive, is overwhelming.

In God's army, nobody is a nobody. Everybody is a somebody. We've learned that lesson. Many of our campaigns hinged on the key contributions of quiet, unknown people. The Lord opened massive doors swinging on the hinges of regular people. Those people are mostly unknown still. But they will be credited at the throne of Christ. How mighty are God's works through unassuming means!

Many times, God's instrument in opening doors was not someone in traditional leadership. They weren't always pastors or committee members. They had little to recommend them as key players other than their simple passion to see people come to know Jesus. They gave the little nudges to ensure that the resting body did not stay at rest. And their efforts snowballed! A nudge from the Spirit through a willing person can become an avalanche of abundant grace.

I wonder if you have been trying to follow Jesus and serve Him solo? I wonder if the individualism of this age, and the constant temptation for isolation that we all carry, has done a work in you to pull you away from others?

If so, consider what it might mean for you to join a group of loyal workers in the cause of Jesus. Perhaps you are a gifted leader with a vision for mission and service. Good! Use that! But do not use it by yourself. Use it to inspire, serve, and embrace with humble confidence the path that God has for you. Perhaps you are called to serve and support the clear vision of someone following Christ. Good! Faithfully work out that calling according to your gifts.

This calling to serve alongside our brothers and sisters is a gift to each of us and to the world.

Through the community and support of colleagues, I have found a way of working together that is so much better than alone.

CHAPTER 9

No Greater Joy

My Sons, Kevin, Keith, Andrew, and Stephen Palau

I have no greater joy than to hear that my
children are walking in the truth.

3 JOHN 1:4

The night Pat's water broke, we were staying in Cupertino, California, in the home of some friends. We were visiting from Portland (where we were living in between missionary assignments) for a missionary deputation at a local church. The two of us had collapsed exhausted into bed after a good but long day. It was January 1963.

Pat was only seven months pregnant.

I was dead asleep when suddenly she was shaking me awake. Her voice was urgent. "Hey," she said. "We need to get to the hospital. The baby's coming."

"What?" I replied. "You're kidding."

"Tell that to the baby," she said dryly.

My heart pounding, I was instantly awake. The clock read just past midnight. The next minutes were a blur of activity as we dressed, woke the family, grabbed what we thought we might need, and got out the door as quickly as possible. We called a Christian doctor we knew in Palo Alto—Pat's regular doctor was in Portland, of course—and he rushed to meet us at the nearest hospital: Stanford University.

Pat was admitted and immediately whisked away. Those minutes were tense. The staff's keep-it-together medical professionalism was somehow more unsettling than people simply acting concerned. I was not allowed to stay with Pat and found myself pacing, praying, sweating, praying, sitting, praying—in the very image of the anxious father.

And with good reason. *Seven months!* I knew full well that lives were on the line, Pat's and our child's. I knew there was a real possibility that I might walk out of that hospital alone.

The doctor returned to update me. "Pray," he said. "You have to."

"What's wrong?" I asked.

"Not sure yet," he said. "The baby's heartbeat is bad. Like this . . ." He drummed out an extremely fast, irregular heartbeat. "I've never heard a baby's heart beat so fast."

We prayed together, my usually confident voice faltering more than once. As he left, I said simply, "If you have to save a life, save hers." I knew the chances for the little one weren't good. He nodded and disappeared.

He came back after a time that felt like hours. "Keep praying," he said. "This doesn't look good."

The clock seemed to freeze. The hours were spent praying and pacing. But finally, at 5:30 a.m., I saw him coming. I steeled myself for whatever news he was bringing but relaxed the moment I saw the joy on his face. "Congratulations!" he said. "You're the father of twin boys!"

I was floored. The crazy heartbeat had simply been two healthy, tiny hearts side by side. "Go down to that window," the doctor said, "and show the name Palau. The nurses will show you who they are."

My overjoyed heart almost broke when I saw them. The flood of love I felt made my concern for them all the sharper. The poor little preemies. They were barely surviving.

But as they grew stronger, my concern faded to simple love, excitement, and a little bit of pride. It was thrilling. I was the father of two boys! In school I'd always been skinny. The other boys would make fun of me and rough me up when we played rugby or roughhoused. I laughed to myself. *Wish my buddies could see me now! Two sons with one shot!* I felt like quite the man.

Andrew came with less drama three years later in 1966 in Cali, Colombia, and so did Steve in 1969 in Mexico City. And so Pat and I found ourselves the proud parents of the best four young sons we could imagine.

Many memories crowd my mind as I remember those years with young boys. How sweet our time was: playing toy cars with them on the floor, coloring or drawing together, listening to their little voices tell me the stories of their day, of their schoolwork, and of the many details that make up a growing life.

While many who ask about our family think of the sacrifice it was for them to not have me around, few seem to understand that loss was mine too. I did not forsake humdrum family life for the glitz and drama of what was "really" important. I had a call and followed it. But never was it lost on me that many of the most precious moments, the treasures of my sons' lives, came and went without me there. I don't regret the choice. I do mourn the many memories that had to be made without me there.

Parenting is a deep joy. It's also a daunting responsibility. Having grown up without a father after the tender age of ten, I felt keenly that I needed wisdom for the task ahead. Though I'd appreciated the example of Ray and other standout men in my life, I simply hadn't had a father to tell and show me what it meant to be a godly dad.

Or had he? I vividly remember one chilly morning when I was six. It was winter and very cold since we had no central heating in the house in Maschwitz. I got out of bed early, before my mother or sisters were awake, and heard fire popping in the woodstove, just barely smelling the familiar, comforting smell of an early morning blaze. I followed the sounds, seeing a little light coming from under the door of Dad's office.

He looked up at me as I pushed the door open. He was kneeling beside his desk, wrapped in a warm woolen poncho. I went in to join him and saw a book laid open before him. "What are you doing, Dad?" I asked.

"I'm reading the Word of God, Luisito," he replied. "When you grow up, read a chapter of the book of Proverbs every day, and you will be a successful man."

A decade later, when I was about sixteen and things were not going so well for us, I remember one time—the only time that I recall—that I got truly angry at God. It's deeply embarrassing for me to admit that, but I have to be honest. Heaven forgive me, but I felt it. *Lord,* I prayed, boiling inside, *why did you take my dad?* Suddenly, I don't know how, Dad's words to read Proverbs popped into my mind. So I began, and there in the first chapter, I read this:

Listen, my son, to your father's instruction
and do not forsake your mother's teaching.
They are a garland to grace your head
and a chain to adorn your neck. (Proverbs 1:8–9)

It quieted me. Not that it took the question away—I'm still asking it. But I felt that God somehow drew closer to me as my true Father through those words. My earthly father had given me a gift by pointing me to my heavenly Father.

As I have read Proverbs throughout my life, it has struck me that there is no better book for a fatherless young man to read. To me, Proverbs pointed me to the One who was there to fill the void left by my dad. Not that it was the same, but God did promise to be a "father to the fatherless" in the Psalms. Proverbs was like a thirty-one-chapter conversation about the real stuff of life and faith that made that promise practical. It was there to help me learn and grow. It helped teach me how to be a father.

How can I be a good father? I would read with that question burning in me, searching for principles. And I'd find them. They were remarkably simple, but I tried to take them to heart. "As a father has compassion on his children, so the LORD has compassion . . ." (Psalm 103:13). *Okay,* I'd think. *I need to be compassionate. I'll work on that.* It was that simple, but it gave me practical guidance.

I knew that, ultimately, I was only a placeholder for my sons' true Father. When the twins were only two years old, one promise leapt from the page at me. To this day when I open my Bible, I see it written in the margin next to Isaiah 54:13: "All thy children shall be taught of the Lord; and great shall be the peace of thy children" (KJV).

I even wrote the date: *10/28/1966. Cali, Colombia.* Sure, the original verse was about the people of Israel. But the principle—that

God's teaching will lead the young to prosperity—spoke deeply to me, and I took it to heart for my boys.

I tried to learn what a man was supposed to be from the Bible. It was the closest model I had—Jesus Christ as the husband of the church and God as our true Father. When it says our Father forgives? Well, that means that I must forgive my sons. I didn't have the option of tossing out a rebellious son, as many parents did in those days. If God did that, where would any of us be? Until I was twenty-four or twenty-five, I simply learned fatherhood from the Bible—especially Proverbs and the Epistles, which contain much fatherly wisdom from Paul if you read just a little between the lines.

I needed this wisdom desperately. The demands of my traveling ministry put unique pressure on my sons and on Pat. To be a husband and father who was faithful, committed, and present would require that I live the principles of Proverbs out.

From the beginning, Pat and I worked to prevent potential bitterness in our sons. We chiefly did this by working to release our frustrations as they came rather than let them build into bitterness in our souls. Bitter parents, even unconsciously, make for bitter children.

I always tried to be sensitive to the unique pressures brought on my boys by being an evangelist's sons. We did devotions together but never in a heavy-handed or legalistic way. Pat and I felt that the surest way to promote bitterness toward God was to make demands on the boys on His behalf. Rather, we preferred to lead by example and with a soft touch. I've heard of some houses that have a "no Bible, no dinner" policy, and I am horrified to think of the bitterness that might sow in the hearts of their children. What kind of God does that strategy reinforce in young minds? God is not the demanding, withholding legalist of so many imaginations. Yes, He asks for all, but only after He Himself has *given* all.

Parenting from the road was a struggle. I always worried about it. Historically, the children of preachers, missionaries, and evangelists bear the brunt of a family's sacrifice, and it often shows negatively in their life. There was no money in those days for the expensive overseas phone calls. It wasn't easy to have long conversations. I often wrote letters to them on the road, but nothing can ease the worry a parent feels in thinking that their Christian ministry may be impacting their children negatively.

Every single time I left, I made it a point to explain why. When they were little, I'd say, "There are boys and girls who don't know Jesus, and I'm going to go tell them about Him." As they got older and were able to come with me on short trips, I made it a point to bring them when I spoke at conferences or camps. I often made it a condition of my attendance—that I could bring my wife and sons. No one ever turned me down because of it. As a result, we got a lot of free trips! These experiences helped the boys realize that ministry can be fun and culturally enriching. You don't always give up. Sometimes you gain!

We also worked to keep the boys involved. When they came with us, they were always given jobs to do. They'd man the book table or pass out badges to the counselors. We wanted them to have a sense of purpose and to learn from the beginning that their involvement mattered to us and made a difference.

One of Pat's great parenting insights was to never make me the soon-to-return disciplinarian. "Your dad's going to get you when he comes back!" was not part of the equation. Instead, she used discipline opportunities to present a united front to the boys: "Your dad and I feel this way." It reinforced the boys' respect for her, and their respect for me as well. And it showed.

I tried to give free rein to my fun and affectionate side as a dad.

I wrote letters to the boys and drew pictures like ones they sent me. "This is how proud I feel when I think about you," I said in a letter to Andrew that I recently came across in my files. I had drawn a big goofy grin. It was absolutely terrible from an artistic perspective, but it communicated that I *loved* my sons. Each of them is so special to Pat and me.

My primary goal was to show my sons our loving God. I'm sure I failed often, but I simply wanted to give them an introduction to the good, abundant, loving God of the Bible. As the years passed, that strategy didn't give us specific answers for many dilemmas. Imagine me raising boys as rock 'n' roll reached its height in the 1970s. Me—raised by a dour church for whom *dancing* was a sin! Long hair? Rock music? *Sergeant Pepper?*

In those days there was a song about Jesus looking beyond the hair to the eyes of a person, and it made a lot of sense to me. If you hunt through our old Christmas cards, you'll find one where the twins have hair just like the Beatles. Pat and I sent it out with a little trepidation, thinking that some of our more conservative friends might stop supporting us. But in the interest of letting the boys be themselves, the hair stayed, the card was mailed, and I think we kept all our friends. Underneath that hair, those boys loved the Lord.

In those days the Beatles were the picture of wickedness in many Christian's minds because John Lennon had said that the Beatles were more popular than Jesus. In spite of that, Keith and Kevin's enjoyment of all things Beatles grew and grew. They even started a cover band, playing Beatles tunes around Sunset High School, where they attended.

Then when they were teenagers, Keith and Kevin went to a

concert in Vancouver, Washington, by Keith Green, a famous Christian musician who later died in a plane crash. He was a good singer and a godly man. Why the Lord took him is a mystery.

That concert inspired a new wave of passion and devotion in the twins. It was a call to consecration and holiness, and the boys heeded it. It was radical. From then on Kevin and Keith were all-in, 100 percent.

When Keith came home from the concert, he took all his Beatles music and gear and threw them in the garbage. (To be clear, Keith Green hadn't asked for that. It was just my son's expression of his growing, radical commitment to Christ.) Keith thought he was done with that phase.

What he didn't know was that Pat dug through the garbage can and saved the albums. She tucked them away for years. At some point, at one family gathering or another, she said, "Hey, Keith—you still like the Beatles?"

Of course he did, and she gave him the whole stack back. At a time when many Christian parents urged their kids to pitch their secular records, Pat saved her son's from the trash! That is a great example of the balanced, counterintuitive parenting that she excelled at. You can see the fruit of her parenting in our sons' lives. Praise God! She led the way, and I tried to join in full partnership.

But the truth is that Pat not only had to be Mom; she's had to be a little bit of Dad too. Nobody trained me for being a dad. Fishing? No. Hunting? No. Fixing stuff? No. I'm useless! Even with the instructions in front of me, I can't so much as fix a faucet! But the boys have learned from their mother. They are all hard-working, creative problem-solvers. She is very practical. She gardens, fixes things, and is handy around the house.

God knew that our family would need a woman with such strength, skill, and the capacity to nurture and foster connection. Our boys are who they are today because Pat has gone the extra mile. It's not about keeping score—ours is a partnership with real unity—but I simply have to say that she gets the credit for showing our boys the love of God day after day, year after year.

One of the hardest aspects of parenting is that you are rarely able to tell how well you are truly doing. After Billy's passing, *Christianity Today* published an article that included statements from his daughter indicating how absent he was. That absence was a point of deep regret for him, of course, but there is no question that his ministry sometimes came at his family's expense.

I saw that in his life more closely than most. Once when we were together at a conference in Amsterdam, Billy got up to speak and began to introduce his family. His daughter "Bunny" turned to Pat and me, who were sitting beside her. "Listen," she said. "My dad's going to mention all us kids but forget me." Sure enough, he did, going through his kids one by one ("Gigi . . . Franklin . . . Anne . . . Ned . . .") and then continued straight into his talk. *He missed Bunny.* It was surely an oversight, but it had happened frequently enough that she had grown to expect it. I understand how it happened, and I am not judging Billy. He was not perfect, and who is? I knew Billy loved his kids. Undoubtedly. You could *see* it. But he admitted to me that he regretted being gone so constantly and felt sometimes that he had failed his kids.

I hesitated to share this story. In fact, I crossed out this section from the manuscript more than once. I was concerned that I would be seen as tearing Mr. Graham down or puffing myself up. Neither is true—and it pains me to think anyone might read it that way. Ultimately, I decided to share it because it shaped me in a way and because Mr. Graham's children have been so public about the ups and downs of their relationship with their dad.

No one is perfect. None of us can be everything to everyone. No matter who we are, no matter how profound our ministry, we are human beings in need of daily closeness to our Savior. It can be easy for anyone to overlook those closest to us.

But Christ can redeem this. Our humanness and brokenness can lead us to the kind of humility I saw so clearly in Mr. Graham. Are you inspired by the image of an unattainably holy Christian superhero or the idea that *any* of us—flaws and all—can be used by God? Doesn't our humanity, including being honest about our shortcomings, reveal God's power? This is what the apostle Paul writes about in 2 Corinthians 4:7: "We have this treasure in jars of clay to show that this all-surpassing power is from God and not from us." Our fragile human weaknesses make us like jars of clay. And yet, cracks and all, our weakness is what reveals God's power.

Yet while there is grace, there is also a call to treasure those relationships closest to us, especially for those in vocational ministry—where something good can distract from what's best, and too often it's the family that is sacrificed. After that moment in Amsterdam, I prayed about my relationship with my boys. I searched my heart. *Am I present and balanced in my relationship with my sons? Am I giving even the appearance of favoritism?* I knew the questions were vital. These relationships were not guaranteed to be healthy just because Pat and I were devoted to Jesus. The thought of one of my sons feeling like Bunny—it would break my heart. Not to mention the heart of whichever son felt underappreciated.

Pat and I worked doubly hard to keep our family relationships strong after that—because we saw we *had* to. We tried to be conscious and consistent. In the end, parenting is God's work, and we prayed to partner in that with Him well. We could not take our parenting for granted.

The Bible, particularly the books of Psalms and Proverbs, is full of the wonder that comes between the generations. In the newness represented by children and grandchildren, there is a sense of change but also of permanence. "Your faithfulness extends to all generations," the Psalmist writes. How true that is. You can learn that principle as a child, but you cannot *feel* it until you grow older and experience it for yourself. How far away my father feels on that cold morning I caught him reading Proverbs by the fire! Yet he feels so close, as I find myself hugging my grandkids, saying the same old stories and one-liners so that they will remember some piece of wisdom that will help them even when I'm gone.

Part of the wonder of the generations is that the old do not corner the market on wisdom. In fact, as I think of my sons, some of the greatest contributions that they have made to my life—besides their simply *being*—is a fresh perspective that my older eyes could not see until they showed me. The older generation certainly has experience. But there is fresh wisdom among those still growing. Just as the young need to listen carefully and respectfully to their elders, so also their elders should listen to the young. Only when the generations truly respect each other's gifts and listen to each other will we all live up to our potential. That's how we all grow and mature.

The boys were the first to suggest that we shift our campaigns toward the festival model—using the gatherings as opportunities for celebration and fun as well as clear Gospel preaching and united church service. I remember when they suggested that we feature skateboarders in our evangelism outreaches. I felt so *old*. I am a grandpa! What do I know about ollies and halfpipes? But they were right. Doors were opened to entirely new groups of people and social subcultures, and we had opportunities to gather more people together than we ever had before. Their insight and ingenuity were right on. But I didn't see it until it was already working. As a dad, I loved that—being able to recognize that your sons have made the right call, even in spite of you!

It wasn't always easy. Sometimes I even *actively* made trouble, with the best of intentions, of course. The best example of this is when I really felt called to go to New York City. This came just as Kevin was transitioning into full leadership of the team. We were still figuring out how we'd work together. I went to him, passionate about the call. He listened diplomatically and then told me in no uncertain terms that we were not ready for the challenge of doing a New York campaign. Going to New York was possible, but we needed significant preparation. Moving too early could be disastrous.

"No" wasn't what I wanted to hear. The old Luis, who could step on people to get what he wanted, flared up. Without consulting Kevin, I led a chapel service for our team that announced—guess what?—we were going to New York City!

Kevin, rightly, was stung. He was leading with discretion and vision, and in one fell swoop I undermined his leadership, publicly announced something we were not prepared for, and hurt my son's feelings. For a few months after, we went through a hard period. We simply did not see eye-to-eye, and neither was willing to budge. We were both committed to the rightness of our position.

I like to think that we both ended up right, but really, that's me trying to feel better. Kevin was right. Period. We went to New York (that story's in the next chapter), and it fulfilled my calling. But my sense of timing had been off. It required a monumental effort that my premature announcement didn't take seriously. Kevin clearly foresaw the effort and took it seriously. We reconciled, but it was a vivid reminder of how hard it is sometimes for us elders to listen to young leaders when they say something true that we don't want to hear.

Holidays are wonderful in the Palau house. Our sons now have families of their own, and gathering as three generations is a delight. We pray together, though like most families we know the grandkids are at various stages in their spiritual journeys. Pat has always been determined to keep the family tightly knit. She has seen so many families whose kids have gone different directions, gradually drifting apart until the siblings are strangers by the time they're fifty. She decided *not on my watch* and realized early on that if determination, good cooking, and Oregon Ducks football could keep us together, she would make it happen. We all vacation together every summer and have parties as often as we can. Andrew and Wendy are often elected as the hosts, but everyone pitches in. It's wonderful. We genuinely enjoy each other.

When my sons were still toddlers, I began to pray a specific prayer for them. I prayed that God would make my sons "pillars of the church, soldiers of the cross, and true servants of God." I deeply wanted them to support, contend, and pour themselves out for the sake of Jesus and His kingdom. I prayed that whatever they wanted to do with their lives, no matter what their calling or vocation, they would put Christ first. Whether or not they ended up in vocational ministry, I prayed with all I had that they would love Jesus and serve Him. Praise God, I have lived to see that *beautiful* sight in the lives of each of our boys!

I often consider what kind of legacy I want my sons to continue. Many things personally, but in terms of our work and calling, my mind always comes back to the church. Evangelistic work is fundamental to the health of the church. Evangelism grows the church, unites it in Gospel mission, and leads it in speaking hope publicly. I want each of my sons to carry and grow a legacy of building up the church with everything they've got.

Kevin's leadership of the LPA team is a godsend. The ministry that we've worked so hard to build is thriving. We work with diverse methods and strategies to build unity in the church, bless our community with no strings attached, and proclaim the Gospel without shame to anyone who will listen. I have learned so much from Kevin. Not that it has always been easy, mind you—we've butted heads more than once. But I have learned to listen to him—not just as a dad but as a co-laborer. Kevin's leadership has proven that his vision is consistently ahead of the curve. He has an uncanny, God-given instinct to see where things are going and what will be needed long before others notice it.

When Kevin, with Andrew on board, began spearheading the change from "crusades" to "festivals," highlighting the joy of the Good News rather than the militant idea of a crusade, I didn't like it. Not at all. I couldn't understand it. I simply couldn't see what he was seeing. He knew his generation and could see something that I was blind to. Often, people with quick minds like Kevin don't realize that others have a hard time following them. It took time for Kevin to learn to effectively explain what he was seeing.

For instance, in Kevin's great work for City Gospel Movements (where the unity from a campaign becomes an ongoing effort of service and evangelism), he looked ahead to what needed to be done. I didn't. In fact, I was afraid. I came from a generation that feared such efforts would involve politicians and social action that would dilute our evangelistic emphasis. But Kevin has been able to lead the church in simple service and remarkable acts of love that are separate from yet support our unashamed work for the Gospel. I learned that the church can be involved in the community without compromising our faithfulness. In fact, it *increases* our faithfulness to simply serve those in need with our energy and resources.

Keith is a low-key man but strong and committed. He isn't the kind of person who seeks attention, but his faithfulness is inspiring. I will never forget once when he spoke in chapel for our LPA team. "I'm not a public speaker like my brothers," he began, but he went on to tell the story of how he has befriended so many of the members of the Portland Timbers soccer team and hundreds of fellow fans through shared charity work in foster care and has become a well-known personality in the Timbers organization. He loves these mostly non-Christian fans and athletes. They open up to him, sharing their hopes and their struggles. They ask him to pray for their marital troubles. It's an amazing thing. And it's just one example of the kind of committed person he is. Still waters run deep with Keith. He has deep personal friendships and elicits a fierce loyalty from those friends. Many of his friends became long-term prayer partners and faithful supporters.

People often ask about our son Andrew and his prodigal season. I don't know quite what to say. You can read about it in his own words in his book, *Secret Life of a Fool*. Andrew was born a leader, and leaders, for better or worse, must find their own path. Those were very hard years. But they are his story. As a Christian parent, you ask yourself if you did something wrong. But you can't blame yourself for choices that weren't yours to make. God gives our kids the same will and choice that He gave us. They get to exercise that choice. We do our best to train and guide them. We try to show them the truth and the blessing that comes from living in the light. But their life is their life.

When you ask *him* about those years, his response is quite simple: "I liked to party." He knew what was right and wrong. It wasn't a matter of knowing. It was a matter of choosing. Even during his wildest years, he'd come home from the University of Oregon with his head full of corrections for all the "wrong" things he'd heard in class or on campus. He'd passionately share something he heard a professor say about Christianity, followed by, "But that's not true, is it, Dad? It's antibiblical!" If I hadn't been aching so much for him to embrace the Gospel, I would have laughed! From the very beginning, Andrew had the ability to spot a phony a mile away. He didn't judge people or pretend to be better than anyone. He simply discerned where they were coming from. He has a quick, accurate theological mind, but his deepest gifting is as an evangelist.

Sharing a festival stage with Andrew is a joy. It is so satisfying for an old dad like me to see the younger generation stepping up. That satisfaction grows exponentially when it's your own son. I don't have the words to describe that feeling. God is so good.

Only the Lord can appoint or anoint an evangelist, or anyone else for that matter. Featuring Andrew more prominently was more a recognition of God's anointing than any decision on our part. It's not fair to Andrew or to me to say things like he's inherited my preaching ministry or somehow taken up "my mantle." He needs to grow and develop his own style, mission, and ministry. I hope that if anyone ever sees him as being in my shadow, the light of Christ will dispel that faster than we can blink. We stand, both of us together, in the shadow of Christ, commissioned by the same Father, anointed by the same Spirit, and preaching the same Christ crucified to bless the nations.

Stephen, our last born, inspires me with his faithfulness and commitment to his sons. He is so fun and relational, making friends easily, and he has a wonderful laugh. He is godly too, keeping his spiritual life vibrant, walking devoted to the Lord. He's been a wonderful elementary school teacher for more than twenty-five years, showing incredible love for his students. He teaches fifth grade here in Beaverton, at the very school he went to, and is an example to our whole family and team. The same drive and excellence that helped him stand out during his four years of playing football at Sunset High School and Wheaton College shows as he uses his gifting to educate and lead others. He has a weekly men's group that faithfully prays and supports each other in a powerful way.

Steve is the life of the party. Andrew is not far behind. The twins, a little softer spoken, are less boisterous. Each of the boys brings a special quality to our time together. How I love them!

My early prayer has been answered. To see each of them walking with the Lord is an incredible feeling, a feeling unlike any other. I love my family so much.

Now the boys are leading the way, each in his own manner. I watch in awe as the Lord guides each of them. I admire the godliness they each manifest. I look at each of my sons with such godly pride. They are men of God. Different in calling, different in their gifting, but each a source of joy and an honorable representation of the Palau name. They each live for holiness, for their family, for Christ. They serve the church and our community in remarkable ways.

When I found out that I had terminal cancer, one source of joy was knowing that the boys are prepared for what lies ahead, both in life and in ministry. My cancer diagnosis meant that I had to fully step away from my leadership roles in the team and as an evangelist. In theory, you want to turn over your ministry. In practice, it wasn't easy until the doctor looked me in the eye and told me I had to. But I see the faithfulness of the Lord, the creativity and drive of our sons, and the many others who work to share the Gospel as part of our team, and I know we are doing more than I ever could. I cannot imagine the future of our ministry, even though the message will be the same. I am delighted to have responded to the command of the one "who began a good work" in me (Philippians 1:6). But I delight still more in faith, trusting that Jesus will guide the next generation of Palaus to lead with the same commitment, generosity, and creativity that my own father exemplified.

As I contemplate the wonder and power that comes when generations share what they have been given for the Lord's service, I wonder where you find yourself. How is your relationship with those older or younger than you? That might include family members, but it certainly includes others—neighbors, church members, coworkers, and many more. Do you dismiss them? Or have you learned the power of perspective that *both* the old and the young have? Do not cut yourself off from what God is trying to give you through another generation's perspective.

We are all stronger when we listen to each other and forget our small and petty differences of opinion in favor of remembering the incredible love and truth that unites us in the cause of Jesus. After all, we all have the same call. We might talk about it in ways that feel as different as the change from "crusade" and "festival," but in the end, only one thing matters: shining the light of the Good News together.

CHAPTER 10

Bless the Nations

The Beautiful Unity of the Church

Christ himself gave the apostles, the prophets, the evangelists, the pastors and teachers, to equip his people for works of service, so that the body of Christ may be built up until we all reach unity in the faith and in the knowledge of the Son of God.

EPHESIANS 4:11–13

Deep in the jungles of a Latin American nation that shall remain nameless, I met three young men. Much like any passionate young fellows, they enjoyed time with friends, liked a good joke, and dreamed of settling down with a special someone. I suspect that the only difference between them and the average teenager was that these young men were never without a rifle and a few grenades. You see, they were guerrillas.

They came from evangelical homes but became rebels, and

although I disagree with their method, they were fighting for a good reason. Everything was upside down in their nation. The military and police had become a merry-go-round of corruption. The injustice had gotten so bad that these young men were willing to put their lives at risk in hope of something better. "Enough," they must've said to each other. "Let's try to change this." So they did.

These kids joined a band of rebels way out in the Amazon jungle. Things didn't go quite as they had hoped, and the revolution stalled into a slow-moving stalemate that just entrenches and makes everything worse. There would be a skirmish here, a retaliation there, potshots at anyone careless from the other side, and never any lasting change.

Their hopes had withered. To cheer each other up, they gathered around the shortwave radio any chance they got. Radio programs are sparse out there. As it happens, I'm on about four thousand radio stations in Latin America. Odds are pretty good that you can turn a radio on just about anywhere on the continent and fiddle with the dial until my voice comes out of the speaker.

I later corresponded with three of those rebels, and they told me their story. "We started listening to you out there in the jungle," they said, "and slowly we started to say something to each other: 'If we ever make it out alive, let's preach the Gospel.'"

Well, they made it out alive. When they wrote, they shared incredible stories of how they extricated themselves from the cycle of violence. Then those three young men began to use the incredible grit and jungle skills they learned as revolutionaries to begin planting and leading churches in the same remote areas where they once packed weapons. Bibles replaced their bandoliers of ammunition. The whole area would be called godforsaken by many people. But He has not forsaken it.

I see my entire ministry—from evangelism to teaching, from broadcast ministry to representing Christians to politicians and world leaders—as supporting the church. Yet one of the main historical critiques of mass evangelism from other Christians has been that it undermines the role of the local church.

In American Christianity, the evangelist has often been seen as an enemy to pastors. Evangelists are often looked down on. Sometimes they deserve it, but there's more to the story than that. Evangelists and pastors should be the closest allies. All the giftings of Ephesians 4 should be working together to build up the body of Christ

I feel that prejudice goes back to the days of George Whitefield, an evangelist and a companion of John Wesley. When Whitefield came to town, he had a bad habit of disparaging local pastors. It was one of his weaknesses. Not that he didn't make a few good points, but the principle was wrong. Ever since, the pastor and the evangelist have gone toe to toe. The image of Whitefield as the mass evangelist has become ingrained in American minds and culture. Pastors think of evangelists as flighty, self-seeking, self-aggrandizing celebrity types. Evangelists look at pastors as someone who has lost their fire. Yes, pastors care for souls, but only if those souls join the church and tithe. Both attitudes are horrible.

Anybody can criticize. It takes maturity to build up. If you want to serve Jesus, show us by doing, not by attacking others. Remember the verse: "Who are you to judge someone else's servant? To their own master, servants stand or fall. And they will stand, for the Lord is able to make them stand" (Romans 14:4). Leave others to the Lord. See that *you* are standing first in your own calling. What does another person's calling matter to you?

Mass evangelism does not have to oppose the local church. Neither does mass evangelism need to be an indictment of the local church. Evangelism is a separate gift of the Holy Spirit, mentioned more than once by Paul. Not all pastors are evangelists. Not all evangelists are pastors. While both need to shepherd Christians and share the Gospel, they have a different calling. In fact, their gifts ought to work in tandem, hand in glove.

People sometimes pit evangelism and discipleship against each other, as if energy toward the one somehow detracts from the other. At this, I scratch my head and think, *What?*

How can you disciple someone who has not been converted? How are you going to teach and train and form them to be like Jesus if they have never committed to following Him in the first place? The beginning steps of the Christian life are the result of a choice to forsake what has gone before and turn to new life in Christ, freely offered. Evangelists work to lead people to that choice, not to choose it for them. There is no way around that choice. Not choosing is itself a choice. The opportunity may return because God pursues our souls with a gracious and patient love. Then again, the opportunity might not. This day, like any day, might be your last.

The evangelist helps lead converts to the beginning of discipleship. The evangelist draws them so that the church can grow and mature them. I heard it said once that an evangelist stands at the door of the church crying out, "Come in! Come in! This is the door!" For the new believer, stepping inside is the end of one journey, but that first step is also the beginning of a new one.

From the beginning, I have pledged that our work would strengthen and uplift the body of Christ. No one has done a formal count, but I venture to say that we have ministered to hundreds of thousands of pastors around the world. Our goal has been to bless and encourage God's appointed shepherds.

I have traveled the world over. I have gone from the lowest slums in the world to the halls of the most powerful world leaders. I can tell you clearly—there is no institution in the world like the church. We are more diverse, more adaptable, more creative, tougher, more committed, more joyful, and more *unified* than any other religion, nation, or interest group on earth.

We have faults, and they are many. *Many.* Those faults sometimes mar the beauty. But the faults do not take away from the beauty. They besmirch us. But the stature of our grandeur in Christ is not reduced. In the big picture, the body of Jesus is better than we think. For all the nastiness some of us inflict on others, the body of Christ can be counted on when the chips are down. The body will be there. They genuinely love you.

Several principles guide our team's ministry and campaign philosophy. One is that we will never get ahead of the church. Local church involvement—evidenced by a city or region's churches working together, pooling resources, and leading the way with our team—is essential.

This local church support is what we were in danger of lacking in New York City when I first let my enthusiasm for that city get the better of me. Kevin was right; we *would* need more time than I thought to do it right. If we didn't let support grow naturally and organically among the churches of the five boroughs, then we would be in danger of going farther and faster than God's Spirit was leading.

But the problem with New York City wasn't ever about the *what*. It was only about the *when*.

The first tug for a campaign in New York came before I left Argentina. At the Bank of London, I always paid special attention to the memos about the New York branch. New York was a hub of action. Employees were constantly coming and going. I was fascinated by New York as a hub of business and culture. Its influence was global.

Right around that time Billy Graham held his 1957 crusade in

New York. That historic campaign lasted three and a half months and drew well over two million people. They say that 61,148 people chose Jesus during the event. Billy's real television ministry began there. I had a special connection to the crusade through a friend, a missionary's son who had unsuccessfully tried to teach me to play basketball. Despite not being any good at basketball (I was too short), we remained close even after he moved from Argentina to Toronto for school.

My friend volunteered for a summer with the Graham crusade in New York. Every night of the campaign, the team published a bulletin detailing precisely what had happened that day: what had been preached, who had been met, how the response had been. Every week, my friend would bundle that week's bulletins and airmail them to me. It was thrilling. He knew my passion for mass evangelism and that I had started dreaming. Those packages inspired me beyond words. I read stories of conversions and of daily events that showed the campaign's impact on the city.

New York had been in my heart ever since. In the early days I had misgivings. My name was Spanish. *Who's going to back the evangelist with the weird name?* I thought. *Graham, sure. Palau? Who's that weirdo?* I was unknown and without money, and New York would cost millions. Speaking to New York City was a far-off dream.

There was something else. I knew that I could inspire Latins. I desperately wanted to see a movement in New York led by Latins, not Anglos. Anglo-led movements were typical, and they tended to not include other ethnicities as well. The perception by many, even among Christians, was that Latins were somehow second-rate. We'd show them! Let the Latins lead something unforgettable in the heart of New York.

By around 2012, the timing was right. I had been on the radio in New York for thirty years in both Spanish and English.

My preaching and name were well known. We began quiet preparations, joining with local churches across ethnic lines and boundaries of wealth. Recognizing that no single group, agency, or denomination could begin to address the city's enormous needs, the Christian community partnered with the city to match church volunteers (by the thousands) with specific practical needs in the city (also by the thousands).

Along with that, our dream was that all the tristate area would hear the Good News. Laying the groundwork took about three years, but the payoff in 2015 was immense. NY CityServe was a massive, year-long service campaign that saw local churches doing much-needed, no-strings-attached volunteer work across the city, culminating in CityFest, a huge celebration and series of preaching events at the city's most iconic locations: Radio City Music Hall, Times Square, Central Park, and more.

Letting the Latins lead was not the most strategic decision in terms of numbers. My sense is that other communities, Caucasians in particular, held back a bit as a result. I think it was subconsciously because they were not asked to be in charge. But I have no regrets. Others simply needed to decide whether they would cooperate to support something that they were not hosting or in control of. Many did! But many did not.

With the city's Latins taking key leadership, many of the city's other minorities quickly joined under the banner of a united Christian campaign—African American, Chinese, Korean, and many more ethnic groups. Everyone worked to stretch beyond their comfort zone and connect in a sense of shared mission. The unity confounded the press, who genuinely didn't know what to make of a patchwork campaign that, despite hiccups here and there, came off quite seamlessly.

Our mission was simple, but the logistics of a years-long ministry campaign were endlessly complex. We were planning events in some of the world's most prime real estate. With so many different communities and churches involved, there were many little incidents of cross-cultural miscommunication that we look back on and laugh. At one point, we held a rally at a Hispanic church in a relatively dangerous neighborhood. The leader of a prominent Korean church was invited as part of the buildup to our campaign. He thought that he'd been asked to speak, but the host church was just intending for him to say hello. He took the microphone and began a speech through an interpreter! The Latins hosting him were shocked but blessed. This bright, capable leader was so eager to participate that he dived right in. That showed an honor for their leadership and passion for this shared mission. What could have been a cultural faux pas turned into a beautiful confirmation of our work together.

I moved temporarily to New York for a few months toward the end of the campaign. The city's energy was intoxicating. Sure, there were frustrations. But like most frustrations do, they simply forced us to think harder, work together more creatively, and adapt. So we did. New York feels like a microcosm of the world. Even though Chicago is close, London is similar, and Paris is incredible, no other city is quite like New York. Two hundred and twenty languages are spoken there. I loved seeing the church pulling together in the city.

The only thing that seemed to hold us back in New York were the city's new regulations since the Twin Towers fell. Every outdoor event was subject to added scrutiny and security measures. Maybe I'm too optimistic, but I expected that we could have pulled half a million people into Central Park. The stringent restrictions limited our gathering to sixty thousand, which is fewer than those Billy led to Christ in New York! (We felt better when we learned that the city didn't even make an exception for the Pope when he came three months later!) We could have up to sixty thousand, and we had to turn the rest away—they could not even gather in the streets. We felt that, given the bustle of the area anyway, the security restrictions were more symbolic than practical. We tried every strategy we could think of. We looked for a loophole. Nothing. For a while, I suggested to our team that we do a very Latin thing—tell people to come in anyway. But it wouldn't have been responsible or honoring to our host city. In the end, we respected the city's desire to keep people safe and decided that we would preach our hearts out no matter how big the crowd was. After all, it has never been about the numbers, as much as we want to maximize every opportunity. I'd also be recorded on video for broadcast purposes across the US and beyond.

As we thought, another plan developed. We could not have one single enormous event? Fine. We would do *many* rather than *big*. Our London campaign was longer, but New York was the largest scale effort that our organization has ever undertaken.

By the end of the campaign, we had held no fewer than 120 events around the city, ranging from that massive event in Central Park to neighborhood events, luncheons for business people, and a gathering at the United Nations. We were on television and radio. We had print interviews, taxi-toppers, subway ads, double-decker bus banners, and two full-page advertisements in both the *New York Times* and *New York Post* inviting people to join us for events and including a clear statement of the Gospel at the bottom. Even reporters who we worried might be biased against the Gospel were gracious. If they had criticism, they held it back, sensing that whatever was happening in the city, this really was a movement. It was bigger than them, bigger than Luis Palau, bigger than any one person or church. It was citywide, and it was *real*.

Andrew and I decided that we would give an invitation to faith every time we spoke—particularly if they were broadcasting live and couldn't edit it! We felt that we were in keeping with why we were in town: not to be pushy in the least but to share what we believed and the simple faith that we believed Jesus was asking them to adopt too.

People were saved by the thousands. Only heaven will tell the true impact of that time. By the time we were done, our best in-house estimates concluded that up to 80 percent of New York had a chance to hear the Gospel because of the total of our activities across radio, television, print media, and more. I don't exactly know what to make of a statistic like that other than to say, "Lord, I wish it had been 100." And with the next breath to say, "Thank you."

There were little scuffles behind the scenes, as you always have when you get a big extended family like the church together. At one point, we wanted to host an event at a local beach where we could have easily set up a fantastic event that we estimated could have reached about twenty thousand people. There was just one problem. On this particular beach, anything goes. That includes setting up a stage and preaching. And, well, *anything else* goes too. This beach was well known for being a place to sunbathe the way that God intended. While I was willing to preach to twenty thousand topless people, some of the local churches simply weren't comfortable with the situation. We went back and forth, not willing to let a good opportunity slip away. In the end, our respect for the local churches and their leaders won out, and those beachgoers were allowed to bronze up without us.

The year passed with literally *thousands* of stories of God at work through His people in the city. One *New York Times* interviewer asked a key question, one that routinely stuck out in the minds of those watching: "How do you manage to unite all these people? All these cultures?"

"Jesus," I said. "Believe me, it's because of Jesus." I haven't come up with a better answer since. Secular people see the Christian movement strictly in sociological terms. Sure, there's a sociological element, but the bottom line is spiritual. It has been from the beginning, when Jesus's followers first preached the Gospel in the incredible melting pot of the Roman Empire and saw their churches swell with every kind of person imaginable. That hasn't stopped. Jesus can still bond us into one family, the rich and the poor, the educated and the simple, from the peoples of every nation. We come together when we come to Jesus. That is the greatest witness this world has ever seen because it is the most unexplainable. There is no accounting for it, and the longer you think about it, the stranger it becomes. Praise God!

No matter what anyone else says, you haven't done New York if you haven't done Times Square. Who wouldn't dream of having an evangelistic event there? That story was one of the most incredible of my career. We asked, and the area authorities turned us down, saying that we couldn't hold an event there. We felt, inexplicably, that despite their firm denial, they were wrong. Times Square would be part of our New York story. We had no idea how, only that it must and it would.

The sticking point was a local ordinance that said that after 7:00 p.m., you couldn't have any sound of significant volume in Times Square because of the plethora of Broadway shows nearby. Nor could you build a high platform. You could only have a one-foot platform. Our teammate said, "No, no—we need a big platform, we need big sound. We have big music, Palau speaking, his son speaking."

"No way," the authorities said.

So one of our team members, an Italian from Argentina named Carlos, said, "Okay, what is this rule? Who set up this rule?" No one knew. They were just there to enforce it. "Well, I'd like to see the rule," he pushed, "because this doesn't sound reasonable. This is a place for all Americans." So the digging began to find the statute.

By the time it was over, it was revealed that there was nothing in writing—no regulation, no city ordinance. "Well, you still can't do it," we were told, even though there was nothing on the books to prevent it. So our team member began asking around: "Who's in charge of this? Who makes the decisions?"

Eventually he got the name of a typical New Yorker. Let's call him Frankie. "If you find him, he probably can work something out," we were told. Our teammate found Frankie. "It's not me, it's my uncle," he said. Ok then. We got to the uncle and asked about the platform. "Of course you can have a big platform," he said. "How big do you want it and where?"

"Well, here, but they say it's not possible—"

"Don't worry. If you let us take care of the sound and the lights, we'll get you the platform."

And that's exactly what happened. We ended up with a massive platform in the middle of Times Square, with music, testimonies, and preaching. The square was jammed, and for three hours the Gospel was celebrated in "the living room of the world." And there was one more surprise in store.

We had wanted to broadcast our event on one of the large screens around the square, but when we approached the owner of our first choice, he said a few choice words to the effect that he wasn't about to rent his screen to no bleeping Protestants.

That made Frankie angry. "He won't rent you one?" he said. "I'll get you *eight* for the price of one." So at about 8:00 p.m. that night, I got up to preach in the heart of New York City. With the lights and the crowds, it felt like the very center of the world, of our culture. And above our heads, as the words of the Good News echoed between the buildings, I saw myself preaching on the screens of Times Square. Not on the one we had tried to rent but on eight more, all better than the first.

Every one of our campaigns has simple yet profound stories like these. The incredible, invisible efforts of others have removed obstacles, found solutions, and allowed me to preach time and time again by faith in God's mighty power. The face on the screen has been mine, but how many people hearing the Good News that night thought of the key people who made that happen? Who knew about Frankie? Or Carlos? I could list so many people who were used by God to do marvelous things. Much of their work will never be recognized. But God does not forget them. And neither can I. I have stood on the shoulders of strong and giving people. It is a beautiful and humbling thought.

"Never in my wildest visions," said the chairman of our campaign, "did I think I'd hear heaven and hell openly preached about in Times Square." *Right there* hearts were saved. Tourists from all over the world were milling about. We alternated fifteen minutes of music with fifteen minutes of message so people could come and go. That way anyone walking by for a few minutes would get the message. The tourists are like schools of fish in the square, walking, milling, stopping to listen. A Wall Street banking executive who stopped by to hear the music was led to the Lord.

In Central Park, the mayor, who was spiritual but not religious, thanked us for our efforts in the city, saying, "I hope this goes on forever." Pastors on the platform came up and laid hands on him. I stepped back, allowing them to pray for their leader. Then an Argentine quartet stepped up to sing "God Bless America," and the mayor was crying like mad. "Wow," he said, "what a song."

Any evangelist is ready for heaven after that.

In my preparation for speaking in New York, I found myself conflicted. I had always told myself that if I ever got a chance to speak to New York, I wanted to use it to address the whole nation. In my mind, I had a historic call to repentance, one that was *given* in New York but *given to* the whole United States. As I prepared, something in my heart wouldn't let me do that. Instead of seeing the nation, I could only envision the crowd. These flesh-and-blood people who would come to the event, who would alter their schedules, free up time, spend money to get across town—were they there for some nationwide call to return to the Gospel? No. They were there because the Lord had drawn *them* personally. They needed me to look into their eyes, not into the cameras. They needed to be the focus, not the backdrop. They needed a simple presentation of the eternal Gospel. Rather than the stirring call to a nation I had envisioned, I wrote one of the simplest messages of my entire ministry. It was so simple it could have been mistaken for any number of other messages from my decades of preaching.

I made three points in that sermon: Jesus came to bind the broken hearted and heal our wounds, Jesus came to seek and save those who are lost, and Jesus Christ came to give us eternal life and take us to heaven when we die. That's as basic as the Gospel gets. I felt peace in that simple approach. I did not want to impress them with quotations or preach from a sense of my own importance or misplaced grandeur. It's easy to sound smart as a preacher, but what does that really do? The audience in front of you is listening for the Good News. Will they hear it? Speak to them! Forget what they think of you.

It was a beautiful night in Central Park. But still, a mass evangelist just sees all the people who weren't there. When the campaign was over, I was a bit discouraged.

It made me consider what my priorities were. This is how things had worked out. Did I think I knew better than God? Of course not. I prayed about it. *Why all the regulations, Lord? So many more people could have heard. So many more people needed to hear.*

The Lord said to me, *Luis, when you get to heaven, you'll be surprised how many were impacted and chose my Son, Jesus.*

Pat and I still attend the church we were married in. Pat's grandparents founded it, so we have a family connection. But we have more than that too. We believe that unless there is a major, *major* reason to go to a new church, one should commit.

Over the years, Cedar Mill Bible Church has been an incredible encouragement to our ministry. We have served as we've been able and have drawn tremendous encouragement from the preaching and the teaching. Al Wollen, the pastor who married us, served us for many years. I will never forget his emphasis on "constant, conscious communion" with God, which helped grow my sense of the indwelling Christ.

What a gift to be part of the body. In both its global and its local expressions, the church is a thing of beauty.

But this beauty is easy to lose in the reality and sometimes in the pain of being around other flawed people. The church is a cross section of the world. Many of our worst qualities are brought with us into the church and sometimes even amplified by it.

Andrew often laughs about a time he was in class with a bright, honest young man who'd left the church—even though he still believed in God. This fellow boiled his struggle down to a simple question: "God, why is it that you're so good, but your followers are such . . . ?" He finished the sentence rather saltily. Funny, sure. But true. Haven't we all felt it?

I sympathize with him, yet I've never been able to turn my back on the church. But as I look around, I wonder sometimes where the church is headed. In the public eye, we have allowed our worst elements to define us. Instead of thinking of the church in terms of light, peace, maturity, service, kindness, and genuine welcome, most of our culture has come to associate the church of Jesus with fear, infighting, anger, smugness, and nasty manners. That's some of us. But it's not *us*.

When I am asked why Christians are so angry, why so judgmental, why they hate others, all I can say is, "I don't know. Ask them. All I know is that anger is not the good life that the Lord promised." Most Christians I know are humble, eager to grow. They trust God, they love Jesus, and they love others, no matter what. They know their faults, ineptitude, and imperfection. The image of Christians as hateful, politicized, ignorant people does not match the majority of the church. Nor should it.

When people push me on the church's racial struggles, I tell them the truth. "In my family we have black people, Jewish people, Latin people, white people, and more. We all love each other and enjoy each other's company. We party together and celebrate. What more do you want me to say?"

If they push me on homosexuality, I say, "As far as I know, three people in my family have identified as gay. One died of AIDS several years ago, one is living the lifestyle, and one is fighting hard as his conscience directs. We love them all. We are family. What more do you want me to say? They know where I stand on the issue. They know my heart." We agree to disagree on many moral issues. Many! But we genuinely respect each other. Love, real love does that. God shows us that.

We Christians are more than bigoted killjoys. Sure, we hold our beliefs close. We debate theology. We can have disagreements. But at the end of the day, we are called to welcome each other like God welcomes us, unconditionally and with open arms. That is the test of our love. That is the test of our Christianity. Christ dined with everyone from the uptight Pharisees to scandalous people of ill repute. Will the Holy Spirit direct us to do anything less? We are to lift high the light. We are to love. He can take care of the rest. Our job is to live and preach the truth. The Holy Spirit will convict the world of sin, righteousness, and the judgment to come (John 16:7–11).

In Central Park, a boyhood friend from Argentina came up after I spoke. "Man, Luis," he said, laughing, "you've preached that message since you were a kid!"

"Thank you!" I said, laughing. "That's exactly what I was going for." The same old thing.

The whole world is in New York. But New York is also in the whole world. Looking out from those platforms in New York was indescribable. Almost every nation under the sun was in Times Square.

Of the many memorable moments from preaching at Radio City Music Hall, there was one image that I'll never forget. An artist who specialized in performance painting, which is as colorful and messy as it sounds, jumped onto the stage as rock music blared, flinging and splashing paint like a maniac. *What is he doing?* I thought. It seemed random and purposeless. His canvas got more and more splattered, colors dripping and smearing together. Then he turned it to a different angle, and the image leaped out at us: the face of Christ, crowned with thorns!

And it struck me that the painting performance was a visual representation of the New York campaign—and indeed the whole church. We seem like splatters of all colors flung from all directions. It seems random, chaotic, messy. Sometimes you may want to give up. Maybe it feels like a waste of time. Or maybe worse.

Then you step back for a moment and see the whole picture. From the blobs of color and the lines that were indistinguishable just a moment ago, you see Someone. You see the face of Jesus represented not just *in* the sprawling, strange body but *through* it. Your heart skips a beat. You see the face you love so much in all its beauty. It's divine and human. It's scarred but beautiful. And you know that you are one small spot of paint that helps make up the portrait.

I want you to know that no matter who you are, you matter. You have something to offer to the body of Christ. The whole world may reject you, but some part of the church will receive you with open arms. Others may deem you worthless or beneath them. We want you.

Yes, we have our faults. A lot of them. But all things considered, I wouldn't dream of leaving.

CHAPTER 11

Be Not Afraid

Delighting in God

in the Face of Death

He too shared in their humanity so that by his
death he might break the power of him who
holds the power of death—that is, the devil—
and free those who all their lives were held in
slavery by their fear of death.

HEBREWS 2:14–15

I have a large painted sign that hangs over the fireplace in our
home. In broad, old-fashioned letters it says one of my favorite
lines from the Bible: *Dios es amor.* "God is love."

This sign once hung above the pulpit of our little sheet-metal
chapel in Maschwitz where I'd worshiped with my family as a boy.
I went to visit decades later. "I always loved that sign," I mentioned
to an elder, remembering the many sermons I had heard preached

under it. "We'll give it to you!" he said. Generously, the church mailed it to me after I returned home. What a remarkable, meaningful surprise!

That reminder of God's love—His pure love, His very *nature*—has encouraged me these last months. I have needed it. When this illness came up, I realized that I had really spent my life forever running forward. I was always running to the next campaign, the next message, the next event. I have spent very little time looking back.

One of my little idiosyncrasies over the years has been to examine my skin in the mirror and look carefully at my hands for any spot that could be leprosy. The question that God asked me as a young man has never fully left me. It reminds me of the struggle that I had so many years ago in considering how far I would be willing to follow the call of God.

How far will I go with God? Out of my comfort zone? Out of my country? Sure.

But how about into disease? Into death?

Having never been truly sick in my life, cancer has led me into a new season of unique though difficult grace. It has brought me to an interesting point of . . . I am not sure what to call it, but "self-discovery" gets close. Perhaps *biblical discovery* gets closer. I've found myself introspective and thoughtful about what has gone before. I have been more present in these months with my family and loved ones. I have been looking to the future.

Most people change the subject when you bring up death. "I'm dying," I say. "Some weather we're having!" they reply. In Western culture we do everything we can to cover up death so that we don't have to see it or think about it. We are oddly superstitious about something that is both a reality of life and an already-defeated enemy for God's people.

But I want to talk about it. It is important to process what you feel and think about at the end of life and how that relates to our solid and ever-hopeful faith.

When the doctor diagnosed me with incurable lung cancer, I suddenly saw myself at the end of my life. This is not preaching about death from a platform. It is all too personal. Whether in three weeks, three months, or a year, I will be walking through that doorway. Suddenly the gaping hole is standing in front of me. *My turn*, I think.

Why lung cancer? It's so unusual. I don't smoke. I don't have answers, but I am seeing some of the fruit of this time. The diagnosis has given me a special grace. I have been given a little time to gain a sense of completion. My diagnosis forced me to step back while still giving me the satisfaction of seeing just how well this ministry can run without me. And I still have quality time to spend with those closest to me.

The process has been healthy, but it hasn't been easy. After it sunk in that I had just heard "incurable" and "cancer" in the same sentence, I went through a period of about four weeks of real soul-searching. A couple months past it now, I can already see that those days rank among the great tests of my life.

I never doubted the truths of the faith. But that doesn't mean I didn't struggle. I spent hours in quiet and prayer. Hours reading the Bible. The Holy Spirit was working in me. People came to mind that I'd hurt long ago, people I care deeply about whom I felt I might have hurt without meaning to.

Additionally, I found myself wanting to talk about death. People who are dying tend to want to talk about death, but people who are healthy do not. People seemed to feel that it would disturb me to talk about it directly. No! I want to. For me, talking clears things up.

During those weeks, I found most of that conversation about death with the Lord. I couldn't talk about it with Pat the way that I needed to. Her Norwegian spirit likes to settle an issue and leave it.

The issue *was* settled. *I* just wasn't settled yet. I needed to process my Latin feelings about it.

When Pat had cancer, she mostly kept her feelings to herself. The boys were in high school then, and they barely knew what was going on! She's on the extreme end of not talking about things like this. Not that she's uncaring; she's deeply compassionate. It's just her personality. (This, by the way, was exactly what I needed in a spouse to balance me out!)

I found myself returning again and again to Hebrews 7–10, that great passage about the heavenly work of Jesus on our behalf. "Therefore he is able to save completely those who come to God through him, because he always lives to intercede for them" (Hebrews 7:25). Those words took on a deeper hope for me than they ever had before.

"Don't you have doubts?" I was asked once by a BBC journalist. To be very honest, I never have. I have never doubted God. I attribute that faith to the faith of others, especially my mother and father. As tested as it was, my parent's faith was simple, strong, and unfaltering. Faith carried them. Faith carried my father into eternity with a song on his lips, even though he had every reason to rage at heaven for being unexpectedly wrenched from his family in the prime of his life. Faith carried my mother through her life, during her grief and joy.

Do I ask questions? Sure. Why did God take my father so young? I'm sure there is a reason. And I'd like to know the answer. Why did Pat get cancer? Why did she have to suffer and battle for her life when she was selflessly giving so much for the good of others? Cancer came. She suffered. She was healed. Okay. . . . What was the point of that? There must have been one; nothing happens by accident. We are left guessing. Or we must simply resign ourselves to the fact that the answer isn't for us to know. A few people told me they were saved because of Pat's story, so maybe she had to suffer for the sake of someone in Scotland who needed to get converted. Who knows? And what about my cancer?

Yes, I have questions for God. But questions are different from doubting. A question focuses on what happened and why. A doubt is about the *who*, cutting at the goodness of God's character. So for all the question marks that I have felt in my life, I have never doubted God's reality or goodness I do not think less of those who have. Times of doubt can serve to strengthen faith. But I have not fought that battle.

With that said, the end of life is filled with great spiritual struggles. The Puritans wrote about it often. Satan accuses, attacks, and seeks to steal, kill, and destroy the work of God in us. The Holy Spirit convicts to restore and lead us to new depths of maturity in Jesus.

Long ago, those who wrote about death observed this dynamic about the end of life. The devil even tempted Jesus on the night before His passion. For four weeks after my diagnosis, doubt did not arise. But my struggle was deep. Even my own salvation felt like it was being questioned from outside me. *You preached to the masses,* the voice of the Accuser said to me, *but they didn't really know you. You have a dark heart, a dirty mind. You hypocrite. You may not even be going to heaven, you who showed so many others the way there.* I swung between feelings of total peace and a troubled heart.

In my youth, I battled sin in certain areas. As I aged, the battlefields shifted. You wrestle with the deep questions more, the superficial distractions less. Simple answers do not easily satisfy. At the darkest times after the diagnosis, I questioned my own forgiveness, which my rational mind knew with complete confidence but which seemed to be unresolved in my heart. I was being attacked.

When I was younger I had no trouble saying, "Satan, go jump in the lake—the lake of fire if possible!" But as I've gotten older, it has taken me longer to realize, *Wait, this is more than a bad day. Something spiritual is happening.* It feels somehow more obvious *and* more hidden.

Our enemy tempts us to doubt and to blaspheme. He attacks us. He comes to steal, kill, and destroy. I remember hearing once that in the Swedish translation of that verse, the word *kill* means "butcher," and I like it. I come from a land rich in beef, and the expert cuts of a skilled butcher come to mind. Satan is an experienced hand at butchering us into pieces, of dividing us and chopping us apart. He has done it to so many people.

The devil tried to butcher Jesus, but couldn't. Because of Christ, Satan has no power to do so against us, even though he tries to convince us otherwise. He reminds us, in an accusatory way, of all the ways we've fallen short of the glory of God.

But delight, not destruction, is the Christian's destiny.

Let me be clear. I know the truth of the Gospel and believe it fully. I have, so far as I have been able, lived what I preached with openness and integrity. No one is above the struggles that come as death approaches—at least I am not.

I hope my honesty about the darkness will help you understand the incredible light and freedom that came when those clouds broke. I did not spiral into doubt or despair. I walked through what I needed to walk through.

There is a scene in Bunyan's *Pilgrim's Progress* where Christian walks through the Valley of the Shadow of Death. He walks the valley at night. He is assailed by evil voices from behind that whisper things into his ear until he is not sure if he is thinking them or not. To one side is a horrible swamp. To the other, a sheer cliff dropping down into the darkness.

When morning breaks, Christian looks back at the path he just walked. The way is littered with snares, nets, and traps. He suddenly and fully becomes aware of God's faithfulness, and he goes on his way to his heavenly destination.

The Shadow of Death should not be underestimated. But we are never alone in it. Christ Himself has walked it, and His Spirit will encourage us through it. The trip takes time. It is not easy. But it is real.

After my diagnosis, one of my brothers-in-law sent me some of the most meaningful notes. The notes drew from his experience of looking death in the eye. "This fire you're going through is not to destroy you," he wrote, "but to purify you." Shadows have real impact, but they cannot destroy you. I was being purified.

I prayed and pondered. The Lord gently replied. He pointed out simple ways that I had become complacent. I was not rebelling in sin, nor had I consciously stepped away from Him. But like boats on Galilee, we all can drift if we are not moving forward. No matter how dedicated you are to the cause of Jesus, if you get careless in your personal intimacy with the Lord, your relationship loses its potency. You're not destroying anything, but you are missing an opportunity for fullness in God's life. You lose the sense of creativity that comes from a vibrant relationship. It can be sin, but for me it was just plain carelessness. I had lost my intentionality, and that was the problem.

Any of us can lapse from a marathon run of faith into a meandering walk and find ourselves suddenly yawning as we peruse the "Verse for the Day" on our phones. I see many old ministers who begin to depend upon their ministry instead of depending on the indwelling God. Pat has often said that taking things for granted is the worst sin we commit. She is so right. How much more so in our relationship with the Lord? How much more with our callings to His work?

If I had taken God for granted, even a little, cancer took that luxury totally away. I needed God desperately. I felt that need in the core of my being. And He was there for me. Hebrews brought me back to a sense of peace and crushed all the competing voices with the joyful weight of Christ's cross. Christ's past, present, and future work on my behalf all seemed to focus down to a laser point. Life amidst death. He endured it all, and even now He was representing me before the Father. I felt my hope renewed as I embraced that in my heart, not just my head, more deeply than I ever had before.

Hebrews 2:14–15 pierced my heart with joy. "That through death he might destroy him that had the power of death, that is, the devil; and deliver them who through fear of death were all their lifetime subject to bondage" (KJV).

Jesus, through death, destroyed the power of death over us. Only that can deliver us into true life. Is that not Good News? We have freedom from our deepest fears because Jesus went deeper than death itself.

We must hold fast to the truth, no matter what we are experiencing. We must rediscover for today the freshness and power of the indwelling Christ. Preaching about Jesus alive in us and about our closeness and delight in the Lord—that's the way to deep fellowship with the Father and Jesus Christ. If you're thirsty, come and drink from the water, the Holy Spirit flowing in you from God Himself.

I am months, maybe weeks, away from heaven. The only thing I can think to say is, "Get close to God." Delight in Him. Let the stream of the Holy Spirit's work carry you to the heart of the Father. In you is the life of Christ, who intercedes for us. How amazing that is! The musty, clinging fear of death dissipates in that freshness. For if Christ has given me His life here in our fallen world, and if He is even now ascended and interceding for me in heaven, will He not be faithful to His promises to bring me safely home to Himself? Will he not bring me into the presence of the Father, at whose right hand is joy forevermore? Will He not let me find the home in Him that I have always longed for?

Life is good. I recommend it. I've had a good run.

Until the diagnosis, I would have told you that there was still so much I wanted to do. But now I think, No, *I've done what I set out to do.* Sure, there are a few things I wish I could have done and a few places that I wish I could have gone. There are a few books that I wish I could have written, and the kind of mild regrets that I think are common for any man of my age—a longing to know, now that this life has so nearly run its course, that every moment, every relationship, every opportunity *counted* in light of eternity.

People are praying that I'll be healed. I'm all for it. But in my heart, I don't think I will be healed. I hear the Lord saying, *Get ready, Luis. It's your turn.* I am not panicked, doubtful, or desperate. I just want to be ready.

You preach peace your whole life. Then the moment comes, and you are facing the prospect of your own death. In a way, I am eager to go. In another way, I hate to leave. Here, at eighty-three, I'm really resting for the first time in my life, although resting has been quite difficult for me. I have appreciated the wisdom of people telling me that it is not a sin to be still. If God Himself rested and commanded that we do too, it must be good for us. But rest has been so outside my personality and habit. I realize now that I've been running for my entire life.

Once the initial shock and subsequent struggles were fully surrendered, a deep and abiding sense of peace replaced them. I never knew I could enjoy such *peace* because of the Lord's presence. The promises of the Scripture have become very much alive. The relationship that the Lord graciously allows me to have with Him is getting deeper and deeper. I'm getting ready to go.

I find myself praying and interceding in new ways these days. I listen more deeply and empathize more readily with others. Prayer seems like so much more than a list of requests for God. Prayer has been an opportunity to join Jesus in the work of intercession for others. My prayer has been deeper and unhurried. It is less about me and more about Christ and His church.

Look to the details, the Lord is saying to me. *Hold your ground. Listen to me. Care for Pat. Care for your boys and your daughters-in-law. Care for your grandchildren.*

When I close my earthly eyes for the last time, I can only imagine what I will see. But I know I will feel at home. It's funny, but you begin to feel almost in a hurry to get to heaven. I am at peace, relaxing, and trusting the Lord. I will leave peace behind me in these last months. "We shall be like him, for we shall see him as he is" (1 John 3:2 NKJV). I have begun to think about what it really means to be like Him and see Him as He is.

As I announced my cancer, people came out of the woodwork to share how something that I had said or done had impacted them. That is a foolproof way to make an old preacher feel humbled in the presence of God. Our Father has done so much with so little.

Since my cancer diagnosis, letters have been pouring in. It's really something to hear from people you haven't spoken to for forty years, expressing some aspect of our ministry that touched them. They talk about their lives, their towns, sometimes their entire region being changed as the result of our efforts.

At this stage in my life, campaigns begin to blur together. The details come into focus when I pause to remember or look up details in the archives, but when many come to me saying, "Do you remember when . . . ," I often realize that what for them was a life-changing moment of commitment or decision, for me has become buried in memory.

"You came and spoke to a group of us dentists," reads one letter I received recently from England. *Dentists?* I think, laughing. *I hate seeing dentists. Why would I go to a whole roomful?* The dentist said, "I was converted that night, and I have served the Lord for thirty years." A woman in the Midwest wrote, "You came one night to speak in our town. I had had an abortion as a young woman and had never told a soul. I felt so guilty. I'd never heard a preacher mention abortion but you did, kindly preaching God's compassion for my pain and His complete forgiveness. I received the Lord, and today have a ministry for women who have gone through what I did." How beautiful!

Part of me thinks, *If they knew me like I knew myself, they wouldn't write such nice things!* But then I remember the people who touched my life in a special way. They were human, just like me, just like all of us. They were not perfect. They struggled with egos, tempers, or impatience. They must have! Part of the beauty and wonder of God's kingdom is that He allows us to be gently refined while living among one another and working for one another. I wonder how Mr. Rogers grew in his faith and sanctification during his decades in Argentina. I remember him as a man with a red Bible. He must have been so much more. Surely he missed his homeland. Surely he struggled. Yet I simply remember him as God's servant.

God has used such remarkable people to bless me. It is a blessing to have been used as well. Part of the depth of that blessing comes because of how *ordinary* we all are.

Over the years, many have tried to puff me up: "Luis Palau: The Billy Graham of Latin America!" What is that supposed to do? Impress people? Ignore all of that. If you are to be impressed by anything about me, then be impressed with this: I'm not all that special. Is that not a greater testimony? God uses the weak. He uses the mundane. He uses the unknown, the small. He uses Luis Palau. He uses you.

I have heard many pastors express a similar sentiment over the years. You minister and pray and teach and bless, but at the end of the day, you still find yourself thinking, *Is anyone even listening?* Many people think that because of how widely I have traveled and taught, I am somehow immune to that question. Ha! Not in the least. If anything, I suspect that the questions grow the more opportunities you have.

For recorded teaching, you go into a small, quiet room. The lights are bright. Everything is sterile and technical. A producer waits on the other side of a glass window, readying levels, ensuring that all is in order. You review the script, painstakingly edited and polished, and begin. It's lonely. It's far from the direct energy of preaching to a packed stadium and nothing like the electric focus that comes when a world leader has tears well suddenly into his eyes as he shoos away his aides, confessing simply, "I need God."

Inevitably, you wonder where the words that you speak will go. Once recorded, these thoughts, these little gifts that God has given you first from the teachings of the Bible, will take on a life of their own. They will be a record of this moment, outlasting your life. They will be copied, shared, and broadcast across cities and jungles. Perhaps they will be talked about in churches. Perhaps they will bring hope to someone considering suicide. They will not be stopped by the walls of prisons. They will not be stopped by borders or jungles. They will go across the radio waves and the digital channels of the internet to people around the globe.

But who is listening? Of all the places those words go, very few make it back to you. True, we receive many kind letters and many encouraging emails. Even still, you cannot help but wonder, *Lord, is this making a difference for you?*

A letter came to me recently:

Dear Mr. Palau,

To start off, I'm not a good writer. I don't always spell right. Please bear with me.

You, sir, changed my life. I'd had a lifelong fear of dying. No explanation why, no rhyme or reason to the overwhelming and complete devastating fear. I'm forty-six now and have done medication, psychologists, psychiatrists. Nothing helped. During one of my particularly bad timeframes of constant worry and petrifying fear, I came across you on the radio and decided to listen. I loved what I heard. I became a regular listener. You comforted me. You soothed my racing mind. I felt like of all the listeners, you were talking directly to me. No medicine or therapy did what you did for me. . . .

I knew God through all my fear, but I still couldn't wrap my head around ceasing to exist. That is, until I heard you. At the end of the day, Mr. Palau, you changed my life. Maybe even saved it.

It's difficult to say "I love you" to a man I've never met, but I feel it's the right thing to say to you.

Thank you.

You wonder if people listen. Then you get a note like that.

It is all right to look back over your life and remember the pivotal moments. It's okay to use them to teach others. But the temptation to live in the past is dangerous. Live for today.

God wants to meet you *today*. Not yesterday, which is a memory, and not tomorrow, which is a mystery.

What happened to me in a chapel at Multnomah decades ago is great. But is Luis Palau on fire for God today? The past is wonderful, but it is only the past. Where is my heart today? Jesus waits for me. Are my eyes turned away from His face to focus on a memory of Him?

I had the sensation of growing up spiritually throughout my lifetime as I followed God's principles and pursued my calling to mass evangelism. It felt to me a bit like growing up as a kid or young adult. As you progress into a new stage of life, you look back occasionally with nostalgia. You know that nothing can replace the freshness of the early years. But we naturally mature. As the years go by, your proclamation grows and becomes richer as your inner life does.

At the end of life, little obediences look different. Today, little obediences look like knowing I'm not supposed to travel even though I want to. I must listen to the Lord. Staying put is not merely about my health or because I am afraid to hit the road. I have been invited to know God in a new way, a quiet and restful way. Rest is opening new aspects of my relationship with Him that will be squeezed out if I keep going, going, going. Even though my human side wants to keep moving, I must ask why. What is my motivation? The still, small voice says, *Stay, Luis. Know me a little better here.* So I try to obey. I sit. I listen to the reading of the Word like I have not done in ages, with a freshness that is given depth by the knowledge that my faith will soon become sight. I listen carefully and personally, not merely to teach others but to be taught myself.

I can serve my wife in this time. So often did I have to leave her throughout our marriage. She is probably well prepared for life without me! I spent fifty-seven years of life on the road, and she has tolerated and supported our shared work with her deep love and grace. But now, in this last season, I must do all that I can to give of myself, to leave her in the best position I can and really *be* with her.

I must listen carefully to what the Lord is saying. I have found peace, deeper than I ever have before, by just *sitting here.* I never thought I would, and most people who know me never thought I'd slow down enough to say something like that. I'm getting invitations from everywhere to speak, to preach, to attend. It makes me feel wanted, loved, and needed! But the truth is that I feel the Lord saying, *Settle down. Think soberly. Make sure that what's needed is done. Rest in Me.* I am dwelling in new ways in the promises of God.

The Lord is overwhelmingly kind to give us the desires of our hearts. All we must do, according to Psalm 37:4, is delight ourselves in Him. That's not too difficult a task, unless we make it harder than it needs to be! Throughout my life, the best periods I can recall are those times when I really did simply *delight* in Him. It is possible to obey and serve Him without delighting in Him.

The famous George Müller, one of my heroes, had this written about him: "George Müller delighted in God." This is such a beautiful description that it brings me to tears. It is the question I ask, nearly daily, as my story winds to its closing chapter: *Do I delight in God?* When we delight in the Lord, He places desires in our hearts that He plans to fulfill anyway. The desires of our hearts become the desires of God's heart. Extraneous, carnal, egotistical things fall away. You focus on the delight.

I am meditating these days upon what I will see when I close my eyes for the last time in this world. While much is a mystery, the Bible tells us a few things.

The truths of Scripture become personal in a new way when you're dying. I have begun to visualize *me* seeing the face of Jesus, *me* entering the rest of heaven, *me* reuniting with those who have gone before. It is no longer abstract or hypothetical. It is "perhaps before Christmas, I will see this. Perhaps before Thanksgiving." I am not becoming morbid. But a special clarity comes from picturing my passage from this life into the presence of Jesus.

Think of it! *How soon I will see His face, the face of Him who died for me!* I will fall before Him with nothing but praise on my lips and love in my heart. What will it be like? What shall I see?

What will my heart feel, my ears hear? I feel like a boy again as I think about the freedom, the unabashed joy, and the knowledge that I have found the source of life itself, in whom all the longings of men and angels find their satisfaction.

How I long to hear His promised words, "Well done, good and faithful servant. . . . Enter into the joy of your lord" (Matthew 25:21 NKJV).

How good it will be! How glorious! Hope will have passed into reality, faith into sight. Only love will remain. Only love!

Forever.

My life verse is the favorite of Mr. Rogers and the one Major Ian Thomas preached on that life-changing day at Multnomah, Galatians 2:20: "I have been crucified with Christ and I no longer live, but Christ lives in me. The life I now live in the body, I live by faith in the Son of God, who loved me and gave himself for me."

This verse contains everything.

I think also of Paul's words in Philippians: "He who began a good work in you will carry it on to completion until the day of Christ Jesus" (1:6).

The One who began a good work in us *will* bring it to completion, but in His timing. He will refine you until your dying day. The more you submit to Him, the more that He can do, in His perfect gentleness and His perfect strength. The more we resist, the tougher He is forced to be. For He is committed to our good, to fulfilling what He began in us.

Life is short. If a thousand years is as a day to the Lord, then our lifetimes are barely more than a blink. Life has so much beauty and so much sadness. I don't understand it. But we do what we can despite our human limitations. We teach what the Lord has taught us. We try to be gracious and to grow in humility.

What do I look forward to most about heaven? Seeing the Lord, first. In my mind I have images, pictures picked up along the way. I know that seeing Him will be something else entirely. Imagine seeing Jesus Christ face-to-face!

I want to see my dad. I tear up thinking about it. Throughout my life, I've wondered if he could see me. Does he know anything about what happened after he left? I mean, I don't want him to have seen *too* much, mind you! I wonder if he was watching God's faithfulness to provide for his family, or if he saw me in Bogotá, London, Portland, or New York. Has he seen the boys? Has he taken joy in his remarkable legacy of faithfulness, generosity, and ministry?

Hebrews says that there is a great cloud of witnesses. I will join them as one tiny molecule in the cloud of faith. To stand beside my heroes and teachers, to say "Thank you, nice to meet you, finally"—I long to meet Augustine, Moody, Wesley, Whitefield. I want to see Billy again, whenever the worship lulls enough for old friends to embrace.

I wonder what mistakes I made that I was unconscious of. What in the Bible did I misunderstand? Where did I superimpose something upon a passage? I will know as I am known, Paul says in 1 Corinthians 13. I am intrigued to find out what that means.

Heaven will be everything we imagined, and more. "There's not going to be evangelism there, though," a friend pointed out once. "What are you going to do with your time?"

"Worship!" I said laughing. There will still be proclamation, just in a different form! We will be praising God for His mighty acts, like in the songs of Revelation. We will be proclaiming the Gospel through praise for eternity.

I want others to see the kindness and goodness of God rather than His harshness. In the early years, my ministry was kind of harsh. I think it was a good thing. You must put the fear of God into people sometimes, for fear is the beginning of wisdom. Justice is justice, truth is truth, and that doesn't change. Facing truth is facing things as they are. We may not like it, but that's the way it is.

God is also the loving Father, the kind Master, the One with greater patience than we can imagine. He is the God of freedom and laughter. Why should we only remember the Lord of heaven when we are afraid of hell? He sets us free. Joy, full blessing, laughter—those are the hallmarks of our relationship with God. It's not just "turn or burn."

In my last twenty years, I have softened even more. Not an inch have I shifted in the truth of the Gospel. But I have become less aggressive, less confrontational. I have been more willing to extend the grace that God has Himself shown me. I've been more willing to meet people where they are and go from there. My convictions have grown deeper than ever, even as I have released many of my more arrogant opinions.

Perhaps if you step back and view my preaching over the course of my life, you get a nice balance between the harsh realities that we have brought upon ourselves through our sin and selfishness and the glory of a God who doesn't want a single one of us to perish.

To be absent from the body will be to be present with the Lord. No more questions. No more fear. No more suffering. No more of the anger, arrogance, and frustrations that dog our souls—everything corrupt and unfinished falls away because new life has come.

It is beautiful.

I have learned lessons in this season of life that I could have learned no other way. God has given me real gifts, even during this time of pain and difficulty. I continue to grow and learn. I continue to be called into God's delight.

Are you delighting in Him? Are you close to the one who has defeated the power and fear of death? Or are you still in bondage to the fear of the unknown?

Turn to Jesus. He is waiting to walk us through the Valley of the Shadow into His glorious light.

CHAPTER 12

Look to the Future

The Hope of Things to Come

I consider that our present sufferings are not
worth comparing with the glory that will be
revealed in us.

ROMANS 8:18

Everything changes in this world except the love of Christ. You
begin to realize this as you grow old.

The basics never change. The Word and the Good News
stand solid. But the Bible is right when it says that our flesh withers
like grass and that even the nations can be blown away like dust.
Cultures shift, customs fade, and generations pass. New generations come and have new ways of speaking, thinking, and working.

It's tempting when you're old to think only of what has been
lost. But Christianity has always been able to look to the future.
Ours is not a religion of nostalgia; Christianity is full of hope and
promise. Never has the Good News ceased to be good or ceased to

be news. Never has there been a generation that did not need to hear the Gospel afresh. Some say, "Adapt or die." I believe that. But it might be better to say, "Adapt and live."

The what, who, when, and where of communicating the Gospel remain the same. But the how changes. We must speak to people's soul in our age. The Holy Spirit lets us do that.

We old-timers must quickly learn to delegate and let the younger generation lead, expressing the Gospel in terms that people understand. For all our stupidity, perhaps the old can teach the young a few things.

My secret prayer for years—which I can share now that I am in my old age—was to influence the church, in particular the Latin American church. Over the years, I have learned to distinguish between what is of the Lord and what is of the ego, but I desperately wanted to bless local churches from the very beginning of my ministry, and that has never stopped.

The church and leaders who brought me up were great on doctrine. Practically, they had flaws—not bad ones so much as *sad* ones. They knew so much that they gave themselves the freedom to criticize others. They had a culture of superiority and putting others down that today I find heartbreaking. If you had heard us talk, you'd think we assumed that we had everything right and were the standard God was using to measure the rest of the church. Even kids in the congregation caught the contagion and looked down on other people.

Self-righteousness was the respectable sin that plagued the Pharisees, and Jesus condemned them more harshly than anyone else. To look down on people is a kind of sin so bad that we cannot dismiss it. (The truly terrible sins of the heart are the ones polite company ignores.) This attitude separates us from each other. It slices and divides the very body of Christ. Those with superior attitudes judge others made in God's image and devalue them to benefit themselves. Is that not so much worse than the passion of an adulterous moment or a lapse into drunkenness?

Jesus chose to be lowly in heart. He placed others before Himself. Ask yourself, when you are tempted to do the opposite, where that impulse came from. It is not from God.

We old men tend to repeat our stories and proverbs. Young people roll their eyes at this, for it tests your patience the fortieth time your grandfather begins, "Hey, kid, did I ever tell you . . . ?" What the young don't realize is that the old *know* they're telling you that story for the fortieth time, and *they want you to hear it a fortieth time.* They are trying to make a point. Don't ignore or dismiss them. I told my sons to always listen to their Grandpa Scofield—no matter how many times they had heard the story before. "He knows he's told you this before," I said, "and he's repeating himself so that you will remember it after he's gone."

So at risk of saying this for the fortieth time, this is the point I want you to remember as you finish this chapter, close this book, and answer your call to follow Jesus and proclaim His Good News: we need to move the focus off ourselves and onto Jesus. That change can only come by clinging to the truth of the cross.

You need to cling to that cross, delight yourself in the Lord, and begin to dream great dreams for him. Not for yourself.

Christ crucified implies the resurrection, the ascension, the glorification, the second coming. When I speak about the message of the cross, that well-rounded message does not stop at the crucifixion; rather, the Christian story begins at it. We live in the work of the cross. If you don't preach that "same old thing" of the cross, you haven't preached the Gospel.

I look back today and wonder. Why, in His grace, did the Lord so bless me with the people who shaped me? I do not know. I think He blesses everyone with wonderful people. Perhaps they aren't as public or visible, but that doesn't make their presence any less real. Will we take it seriously when the Lord puts such people into our lives? Do we consider others a true godsend?

Do you remember the people who have shaped you? Who has pointed you to Christ, perhaps giving more than you ever appreciated? Thank God for the people who do this for all of us! And may we all be inspired to be faithful like that.

When you look back on your life at the end of it, you ask hard questions. *What do I regret? What would I do differently?*

Though I regret my many stupidities and sins, I have no regret in pouring out my years, from the time I was a boy, for the sake of the Good News. If I was given a thousand lifetimes, I would dedicate them all to the same calling. I am so glad I lived that way.

At the judgment seat, in the middle of all my stumbles, this much I know I will be able to say to the One seated on the great white throne: "I obeyed you, Father. You said go, and I went."

I went. He went with me, every mile. And it was worth it.

I love the sentiment of one old writer who describes rising daily, going to his window to look at the sky, and thinking, *Perhaps today, Lord. Perhaps today.* One lives differently with that mind-set. It sets you on fire for Him.

I have a passion for people to remember the second coming. I've heard that there are about three hundred mentions of the second coming in the Bible. That makes me think we ought to pay attention to them. God must think Jesus's second coming is important to think about. Jesus is coming back! There is a crown for "all who have longed for his appearing" (2 Timothy 4:8).

Much damage has been done by an overobsession with the details. The timing and sequence of those coming events are interesting for sure, but do we really need to know them? No. The point is not to create a complicated timeline of how and when. The point is to remember the *who* and *what*: Jesus returns. He is not finished with us. Shouldn't we remember that? Expect it? Celebrate it? We don't have to keep stumbling forward through history. Is this our best—for refugees to keep being bombed, for evil people to oppress the poor? No. There is better to come.

Jesus is coming to judge the living and the dead. Focus on living today—this day—expecting Jesus to return. To do so brings hope and readiness to the body of Christ. The second coming is not abstract theology. It changes how we live. The Son of God is returning to lead us home. Every knee will bow. Every tongue will confess. That is *real*. Believing that doesn't make one an idiot. It makes one hopeful. Jesus is coming again. Rejoice.

I see great hope for the church. I believe that the coming years and decades could bring the biggest harvest that history has ever seen for the kingdom. The generations that I see rising have a lot of good people and genuine leaders. I must accept that they say things differently than I might, and that's okay. I said things differently than my parent's generation.

But what's needed for the church to move forward is listening. I've heard it said, "If you think you're hot, you ain't." Never is that so true as with Christian leaders. You may have some bright ideas, young buck, but you're going to burn the woods down if you don't pay attention to wise voices around you. Imitate our faith, ignore our baloney, and live out your calling.

As generations connect, the Holy Spirit works. Wisdom and

experience flow to the young. Fresh ideas and passion flow to the old. The exchange strengthens the fabric of the church. Wisdom comes from all experience. The interpretations of the elderly aren't always correct, but our experience can still teach you, even if it is too late for us.

In 2008, I returned to Buenos Aires for a historic campaign. I will never forget the crowds. Any person in his own country would be humbled. More so for me, as I had known many of the leaders helping to organize the events since we were teenagers.

When we were young, we all dreamed of Argentina changing. We prayed for our country to move away from corruption and toward Jesus. We longed to see millions of believers in the streets, to see our evangelical faith respected. It was powerful to see a municipality invite Andrew after I had experienced that same town's disdain as a young street preacher.

The president of the nation supported us; the owner of channel 5, the major TV station, broadcast the events live from helicopters for twelve hours a day. We could never have planned this, but here they were. Free!

We have seen great changes in Latin America. I cannot take credit, obviously, but I know that our work and words have been used by God significantly. Seeing biblical principles begin to bless nations is astonishing.

When I left Argentina in 1960, I thought, *I will not come back to do ministry until there is enough proof that God's hand is on us.* A prophet is without honor in his own country. I feared being dismissed. "Who is Louie Palouie? My buddy from college? Ha! *That* guy?" When we eventually came, the timing was right. We had gained people's trust.

When I first went to Guatemala City, there were about forty evangelical churches. Today there are around three thousand. Not every church is mature, but we have started a good work.

My teaching continues to be the same old thing: the oneness of the body, the sufficiency of the work of Christ, the insistence that He died as our substitute on the cross, and the power of His indwelling Spirit.

Our success is not because of me. It's because we've worked faithfully for God for sixty years. We have bombarded Latin America with five thousand radio stations every day. Catholics voice their support, saying that they appreciate learning about the Bible and a relationship with Jesus. We have even heard kind words from atheists, who say that my voice has become a symbol of morality and freedom in the face of corruption or cultural despair. Government workers talk about listening to me in their grandma's house and carrying principles with them into work.

I have always stayed out of politics. I don't believe in politicians who ask for your vote because they are Christian. That only sets us up for disappointment and potentially dirties the name of Jesus in the public eye.

Castro and others saw the choice much like I did—evangelicalism as an alternative to violent revolution. But they misunderstood us, thinking evangelicalism was a political movement. It isn't. If someone says it is, what they are espousing is a counterfeit Christianity. It's a righteousness movement and impacts nations indirectly. It's bigger than worldly justice; it's godly righteousness. Christianity says that righteousness and change come not through killing your enemies but through living in the light of God.

There is a harvest waiting around the world for those willing to obey and gather it. I have seen it in every country, on every continent. I'll never forget being in Hong Kong in 1997 (the second time we went there), as the people of that beautiful island prepared for an uncertain future under Chinese rule. Into a packed stadium I spoke, much as I had a decade earlier in the same place: "Look at the sky! Look at those stars! Look at the moon! Do you think those happened by accident?" Necks craned, and half the crowd came forward. Just as in 1987, *thousands* accepted Jesus in one night. People were *running* to confess Christ and find rest for their hearts.

This is Good News of great joy for all people. Does it get better than that? But we seem to make that Good News hard on purpose. Are we so stupid? We are just not presenting the Gospel for what it is worth. I read 1 Corinthians 13 recently. It pierced my heart with its conviction and beauty, as it always does. "Love is patient, love is kind. . . . It keeps no record of wrongs" (vv. 4–5). That passage has always chastened me. The description of love is what we all long for but so rarely find. That love, from God to us, is the Good News.

Why do we seem embarrassed by the Gospel? Might it be that deep down, we've failed to embrace it as Good News? Why would we hold back? So many of us, I feel, simply say we believe it, but it has not penetrated our hearts. It cannot go *out* from us with conviction because it has not gone *into* us with conviction. Our hesitation is a clear statement of our theology. We pay lip service, but our lack of action reveals our unbelief.

Proclaiming the Gospel is just saying the Good News: "God loves you, He has a plan for your life. If you are honest enough to repent and believe, you will be forgiven and become a child of God. He will never leave you, He will live within you, and when you die, you will go to heaven." That's a pretty good deal. Why not proclaim it? It is not your job to brilliantly persuade, merely to joyfully present.

If you have a vision in your heart, don't give it up. "Never doubt in the dark what God told you in the light," V. Raymond Edman said. If you feel His fire inside, the Lord may be doing all kinds of things in His perfect timing that will make you ready when the door opens, and no one can shut it.

Many of my secret dreams were answered. Few knew about those dreams outside our inner circle for fear of the criticisms that come when you meet with political or cultural figures. I have been criticized by the right for meeting dictators on the left and criticized by the left for meeting dictators on the right. We led several presidents to faith in Christ. Their lives changed. Nations were quietly influenced through quiet prayers and secret dreams. The Gospel for the poor is also the Gospel for the rich and powerful. Because they're all just as poor when it comes to what matters most. And often the wealthy and powerful are the poorest.

I once met a general in a country that shall remain nameless. He had seized power from a corrupt government by force but now seemed (to me) to be in danger of repeating many of the former administration's mistakes. We met. His bluster and bravado were notable in our meeting. Eventually, he asked his aides to leave, and the two of us were alone in his presidential office.

"I act tough," he said. "I act like I know what I'm doing, how to run this country. But you know what, Palau?"

"What?" I answered.

"On the inside . . ." He paused, looked out the window. "On the inside I am a small, scared twelve-year-old boy. I need God."

In the end, we all are simply people. We have the same needs, the same fears, the same sins. And we're all hungry for the same Good News.

There's an old hymn I love: "Lift High the Cross," by George Kitchin.

> *O Lord, once lifted on the glorious tree,*
> *As Thou hast promised, draw the world to Thee.*
> *Lift high the cross, the love of Christ proclaim,*
> *Till all the world adore His sacred name.*

Lift Him high. Proclaim until the whole world adores Him, drawn by that vision of the crucified Jesus, who is perfect in mercy and love.

The Great Commission is not impossible. It is not ridiculous or stupid. Playing a part in nations turning to Christ is not a bombastic, egotistical dream. *It can happen.* Jesus said go into all the world, and He meant it.

I long to see this generation move the hearts of millions of people. Two thousand years have gone by, and we still haven't finished the job Christ gave us.

Are we afraid of the Good News? It seems that way sometimes. Why do we always feel that we have to walk into a room with a baseball bat and knuckledusters? It's as if we're looking for something to fight about. We can see that behavior in the Bible, but it's sure not from Jesus. It's the hallmark of a Pharisee.

We feel like making another person bleed inside is going to soften them to the news that their Maker loves them. Really? The Holy Spirit convicts as He applies truth. Your job is not to take His over. In fact, taking over for the Spirit is the grossest kind of idolatry. Your job is simply to tell the truth in love. To help them feel that maybe, just *maybe*, there *might* be something to this whole "love of

Jesus" thing. Yet we seem more afraid of letting the Good News be good than wading into a fight.

How do you get a passion for the lost? R. A. Torrey said that you need to not only *know* what the Bible says about the separation of the lost from God but *believe* it, letting it lead you to prayer and action. The crisis of the current generation is not a crisis of knowledge but a crisis of belief. In half a second we can pull up any verse, commentary, perspective, or sermon onto a screen in front of us. Now that's convenient! But once there, what is done with that truth? Too often, nothing is done. The idea is sampled like wine at a vineyard tasting—swirled in the mouth, noted eloquently, like a connoisseur of doctrine, and then simply spat out. "Wow! That's great!" But has it gone *into* you? Has it touched your heart? Or have you merely sampled it and now moved on to the next novel idea?

We need to believe, not merely to know. We need to take truth and let it change us. We will never have true compassion for the lost, no true commitment to the Good News, *if we do not believe it*. This seems painfully obvious. But I ask you, if you really believed what you say you do, would your life change? Isn't life the truest test of belief? All too often, our lives are so divided, so segmented, that we can smile and nod at the Gospel and then go about our routine as we always have, without more compassion and without the slightest sense of urgency for those who are sinking into meaningless despair.

Truth is vital. It is not relative. America's most destructive export of the recent decades is the idea that the truth is a shifting, malleable commodity. Today we see this more clearly than ever in our politics and national life—people at the highest levels having the gall to claim "alternative" truths. Perspectives may be different, sure. But truth is truth. Period. If that objectivity is lost, all that remains is propaganda, people trying to use others for their own ends.

There's an old story about three men working side by side in a quarry. Each man was working on an identical stone when someone wandered by and asked, "What are you doing?"

"I'm just chipping away at a rock for a few bucks," the first said.

The second said, "I'm making a nice, clean block out of this rough stone."

The third looked up from his work and said, "I'm building a cathedral."

The were doing the same work, but their perspective made all the difference. With every strike, no matter how tiny, we are building Christ's *church*.

Even so, we have no idea of the repercussions of our work and witness. I can't wait to get to heaven and see the true impact.

Many people have expressed their feeling that they owe their conversion to my work. But I owe my life and work to others—many others. And they in turn only ministered for Jesus because they themselves had been influenced, inspired, and trained by others. We could trace generations upon generations of ministers back through time until, inevitably, the trail would lead us to twelve men who spent three years together in Palestine, walking and working with a man from Nazareth.

Yes, to Him is where all the credit goes—not only because of His Spirit which lives and works in us today but because the chain of conversion and discipleship has been unbroken through the generations. We all owe a debt to those who have gone before, but the initiator of it is Jesus Himself. We carry His Good News, His ministry, and His heart for all souls and all nations. We are part of His movement. And we pray that we might be faithful to pass along to others what has been given to us—the message that God's love is here to bless the nations, beginning with *you*.

Proclaiming the Gospel doesn't mean walking around with a sermon prepped and stuffed into your back pocket. It's much simpler than that. It's my mother, smiling and sharing the truth over steaming coffee in her house in Argentina.

It is a wonderful time to be alive and ministering to the world. I see young pastors growing, dedicating their lives bravely to the mission of the Gospel. I see young evangelists, as creative and adaptable as ever, seeking new ways and means to take the Good News to bless the nations.

The young have a hunger for the voices of wise and open-minded elders, but they also have the strength and bravery to forge a new way, often one more faithful to the Bible than the last few generations have done. I am very encouraged. There will always be advances and reverses in church and culture. But the Good News remains good. For all our faults, God's people remain the salt of the earth and the light of the world.

Deep down, everyone feels unworthy. We should speak to that part of a person, not to their façade or the mask that they're putting on. We need to speak to that small, childish, unworthy-feeling place in their soul that Jesus wants to save and love. The worth and joy of life in Christ will pull them in like a magnet.

Every sin and problem we fall prey to is just another way of covering up our pain. Our relationship with God must be set right. Our agony at being separated relationally from the One who made us brings us the torment that we seek to numb and the brokenness that hurts others. We are lost. We need to let our heavenly Father find us. This Good News could change the world.

How can a boy from a small town in the southernmost country in the world have ended up here? Great things can happen through you even if you come from somewhere small or remain relatively unknown throughout your life. You never know your influence.

Your role is to simply obey the Lord Jesus Christ and follow His principles for your life. From there, who knows how or when or where you will find yourself used by Him? Your story is not only yours; your story is His story as much as mine ever was. Give Him your life. Give Him your story.

Our culture today faces monumental challenges. Why are so many young people struggling with depression? They should be having fun, experiencing their freedom. Yet they are medicated in droves because they are haunted by the very real specter of depression. What has imposed this on them? Why are we divorcing at such rates, bringing misery, financial complication, and heartbreak to families? Sometimes there are good reasons for divorce, like when a marriage is broken by infidelity or abuse. But what is happening? We could go on and on with the sufferings of our day.

There must be a way out. If the Lord can save us from hell, can't He save us from the pressures of this life? He may not take them away, but He can give us the strength to bear them. Can't we choose to live for today and say "phooey" to what others think? Can't we choose joy and faithful living in Jesus?

Of course we can. And you are part of this solution. You are gifted by God. You matter. Whether you have been a Christian for a century or you gave Him your life today, you must give Him not only your love but your *life*. Little obediences open big doors. When God says to walk through a door, you must do it. He will never force you. You just never know what's on the other side.

Your dream may not make history as the world sees it. Even the people around you may not really recognize it. But what you do for the Lord *is* great, no matter how small it looks. Nothing is more fulfilling than following His call. And in the end, who gives a rip about acclaim from anyone else other than our Creator?

Let Him light you on fire with the Good News of Jesus today.

A Life on Fire

The great mystery of the burning bush was not that it was
aflame, but that it was not consumed. Though my body is
slowly failing me—burned out and burned up—my spirit feels
that it is burning more hotly and brightly than ever. I have no
regrets. A life on fire, after all, is a life well spent. My life has been
spent for the Gospel. But it has not left me just some old heap of
ashes. Yes, I am dying. But I am *alive*. I have burned. But I am
not consumed.

As I finish this book, I am realizing that I will not be able to
travel to Bogotá, Colombia, this fall. I am too weak. It has been all
that I can do to simply stand and preach recently. For the first time
in my life, traveling seems out of the question.

I am sad that I will not be able to return to the place that our
mass evangelism ministry truly began back in 1966. I am sad that
I will not be able to walk up the steps in the Plaza de Bolivar and
speak one last time into a microphone, raising echoes from the
nearby streets, and putting the attention of one last great crowd, for
a few minutes, where it should be: on the infinitely loving heart of

God. That sadness only gives me more energy for this moment we share right now.

Will you indulge an old evangelist by imagining with me that we are together in Bogotá right now? The tens of thousands of people who would be pressing around all drop away. There is no need for a microphone, for we could just sit on the stone steps under the Colombian sun. There would be no stage, no music, no banners, no bright lights. Just the two of us and the truth.

I would tell you the wonder of what it feels like to be dying without fear. I would tell you that Christ has been the best of friends and masters to me. Never once has He failed or abandoned me. Not at my poorest. Not at my loneliest. Not at my most stubborn or arrogant or hard-hearted. I would tell you that I see His work at every turn of my life, faithfully providing.

And it is in that provision that I would tell you the most important words I could find to say. God has provided, through Jesus, a way for you to come home. Every sin of yours will be forgotten. Every wickedness washed clean. Your every wound can be bound up and allowed to heal. He promises you "strength for today and bright hope for tomorrow." It is real. It is good. All that you must do is go to Him on the cross. All that you must do is say "Yes" to free salvation through His blood.

Romans 10:9 says, "If you declare with your mouth, 'Jesus is Lord,' and believe in your heart that God raised him from the dead, you will be saved."

If you wish to do this, right now, simply pray with me:

Father, I confess I have fallen short of Your glory. I repent of my sins and ask for Your forgiveness. I believe that in Your love You have not left me to death and loneliness. I believe that Jesus Christ died to bring life to me and to the whole world, and that You raised him from the dead.

Please wash me in His blood, forgiving all my sins. Please fill me with your Holy Spirit and make of me a new creation. Please give me the assurance of eternal life.

I ask this in Jesus's name.

Amen.

It is in the hope of heaven that I write these final words to you, dear reader, the words my father whispered from the pillow that cradled his dying head: "I am going to be with Christ, which is better by far."

I hope with all my heart to meet you there. It will be glorious.

Acknowledgments

To my wife, Pat, thank you for everything. Your love and care during this time has showed the love of Jesus to me.

To our sons, Kevin, Keith, Andrew, and Stephen, and my daughters by marriage, Michelle, Gloria, and Wendy—I am so proud of each of you. You are each a joy to me.

To my beloved grandchildren—you are a new generation, each of you finding your way. I love each of you with my whole heart and am so proud of you all.

To my sisters, Matilde, Martha, Ketty, Margarita, and Ruth; to my brother, Jorge; to my brothers-in-law JC Ortiz, Ed Silvoso, MA Pujol, and Eric Green; and to all my other beloved family across the globe—I love each of you very much and am so blessed by our many memories together.

To our Luis Palau Association team, especially the longstanding team members who have given so much, including John Ogle, Doug Steward, David Jones, Jim Williams, Anne Scofield, Jay Fordice, Carmela Tosoni, Jane Stradley, Debbie Bailey, Colin James, Joy Bongiorno, Scott Kraske, and the many hundreds I do not have space to name. You have been team members, staff, volunteers, and friends over the decades—you have all worked hard, spending yourselves freely for the sake of the unreached. Thank you. To serve with you has been one of the great honors of my life.

To our Latin team—you have sacrificed like few to bring this message to the world. You see yourselves as missionaries, and so you are. I have seen you do near miraculous things for the kingdom and cannot honor you enough. We are already seeing the fruit of your labor. So thank you, especially Ruben Proietti, Carlos Barbieri, Jorge Scopazzo, Edmundo Gastaldi, Jonathan Proietti, and Marta de Hotton.

To all who have served on our boards of directors throughout the years—you have shared your life, wisdom, counsel, and time. You have brought the best of your professional skills to our ministry, always gentle, clear, and biblically centered. You have been incredible co-laborers. Thank you. You have helped make this team what it is, and you deserve to be honored: Scott Cahill, Simon Berry, Howard Dahl, Vickie Foster, Scott Hanson, Mita Jash, Ross Lindsay, Richard Luebke, Mark Neaman, Rafael Pedace, David Reisenbigler, John Southard, Gail Stockamp, George Mackenzie, Lady Susie Sainsbury, Colin Saunders, Mick Spratt, Jack Cauwels, Tom Chambers, Sam Friesen, Robert Gluskin, David Hall, David Hentschel, Lawrence Hoke, Gerald Horn, Wayne Huizenga Jr., and Fred Sewell.

To the many donors and ministry partners who have given sacrificially to see this work go forward—thank you.

To the many pastors who serve, visibly and invisibly—you have the most important job in the world, to feed Christ's sheep. Thank you for all you have done throughout the years in partnership with your churches.

To my fellow evangelists, the men and women who are called to evangelism in this generation and the future—you are carrying the Gospel forward so well. Especially to those we have partnered with in campaigns: thank you for your inspiration and example.

To Paul Pastor, my co-writer and now a friend for life—it has been an honor to work with you. Your skills as a communicator, your gifting as a writer, your godly heart and love for the Holy Scriptures have all blessed me greatly. You have become a true friend. The Lord will be with you powerfully in the upcoming years.

And of course, I acknowledge my lord, Jesus Christ, in all these things and many more. You have never failed me. You are truly Good News. I love you, Lord Jesus, with all my heart.